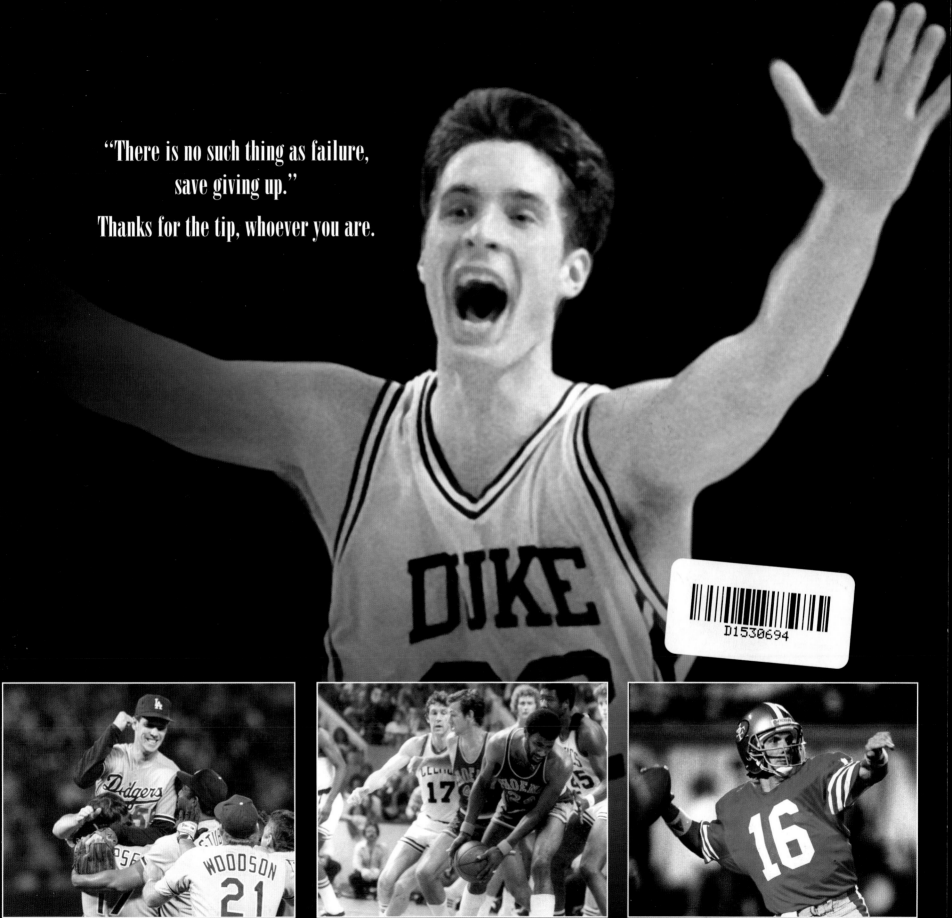

"There is no such thing as failure,
save giving up."

Thanks for the tip, whoever you are.

C O N T E N T S

CONTENTS

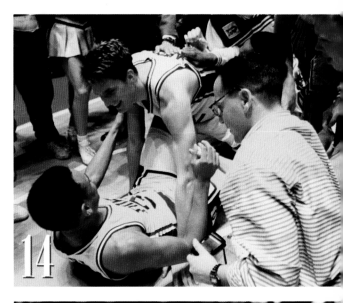

C O N T E N T S

C O N T E N T S

Foreword

The final moments of a tight game can be thrilling to relive. Still, I didn't think my "Hail Mary" pass to Gerard Phelan would be remembered as one of the greatest moments in college football history. I *did* think it would be something my teammates and I would all remember for the rest of our lives. Looking back on my college career, I want people to remember the things we did at Boston College and that I won the Heisman Trophy—not necessarily the pass. But the legend of coming from behind with only 28 seconds on the clock lives on.

Obviously, that play was a big deal to us. By the time we got home to Boston, there were thousands of people at the airport and they were making such a big deal about it. Then all of a sudden you realize, "You know what, this was national TV, it was Thanksgiving weekend." I think all that added to the fact that it was a great game. That's what has made it as big as it has been.

The essence of a big play when you're behind is what goes on in your head right then and there. At that moment, I knew we had to make a big play to win the game. We had done it successfully before, so I didn't think it was impossible.

We all knew it was going to be the last play of the game, so we knew what the play call was going to be. They sent one of the young guys onto the field. I kind of waved him off because I wanted to leave Troy Strafford on the field. I didn't know Troy had a pulled hamstring at the time. But Troy stayed on the field anyway and we lined up. When we went to snap the ball the first time, there was a whistle and a flag and then they ended up picking up the flag. As we realigned for the second time, the guy that was on Gerard decided: "I'm going to walk over and get on [another player] instead," which allowed Gerard to get open and to be the first one down the field.

Basically you drop back, hang on to the ball for as long as you can, and throw it. But I always liked to scramble off to the right and get a little closer to the throw. The offensive tackle obviously didn't know this, so I almost got sacked getting around the corner. I wanted to peak backside at the tight end down the backside boundary, but I didn't have time (someone was running at me), so I just let it fly in that direction. Not specifically to anyone, just in that direction.

I saw a big pile go up. The ball went over two defenders' heads and I just saw everybody fall to the ground and I assumed it was incomplete. There was probably a half-second delay to a second delay before I saw an official's arms go up in the back of the end zone. I was kind of chuckling to myself and running toward the pile.

Lots of gridiron miracles have happened since that fantastic moment in 1984, and heroes have come and gone. Thanks to Gerard, the Eagles, and the fans who can't forget a great play (and it truly was), I have something that people can identify with me. Two, three years after you retire, you're forgotten. At least that's something people will remember and have remembered for years.

The one big thing people didn't know is that the Heisman voting was basically in by then anyway. That pass did not win me the Heisman. I think Joe Bellino said at that time that I had pretty much already won the Heisman anyway.

Though the trophy's certainly a treasure, a spectacular, game-winning play in the clutch is what makes fans return to the stadium. That's what makes football great—and all of sports, for that matter: hoping to see a miracle. . . . And sometimes the right decision, at the right time, can make it happen. This book is about those decisions and those moments and the other miracles that keep fans coming to sports events of every stripe.

—**Doug Flutie**

First Team

The Shot Heard 'Round the World

October 3, 1951, Polo Grounds, New York

The fat lady was all warmed up in the fall of 1951, ready to sing for the Brooklyn Dodgers, a shoo-in to win the pennant as late as September. But the Giants' Bobby Thomson wouldn't have it. By Game 3 of the playoffs, he would change baseball history with perhaps the biggest hit ever in the game. It would be—as the world came to know it—"the shot heard 'round the world." And it never stopped resonating, not even today.

The Dodgers had a comfortable 13½-game lead over the Giants as far into the season as August 11. The Giants were in last place. This was a Giants team that had started the year 2–12 with a deflating 11-game losing streak before April was even over.

The last six weeks of the 1951 season was one long, thrilling Giants comeback. Starting with a doubleheader sweep on August 12, the Giants ran off a 16-game winning streak that lasted until the 28th. Winning their last seven games, too, they were 37–7 through the end of the regular season, 6–1 in games against the Dodgers. With but two games remaining, the Giants pulled even with Brooklyn. Both teams won their final two games, and a three-game playoff was set.

The Dodgers won the coin toss and chose to play the first game at Ebbets Field. Bobby Thomson and Monte Irvin both hit home runs in Game 1, and Thomson's two-run shot off starter Ralph Branca was enough to give the Giants a 3–1 victory as Jim Hearn out-pitched Branca. The Dodgers dug in and crushed the sleeping Giants in Game 2, 10–0.

Game 3 was a pitchers duel for the first seven innings, with the Dodgers clinging to a 1–0 lead into the bottom of the seventh. The Giants came back and tied the game, 1–1, on a double by Irvin, a bunt by Whitey Lockman to push Irvin to third, and a sacrifice fly to deep center by one Bobby Thomson. Like Popeye after a spinach transfusion, Brooklyn immediately responded with three runs in the top of the eighth off Sal Maglie. Suddenly it was Dodgers 4, Giants 1, with just three outs remaining. The situation seemed hopeless, all appeared lost, the great comeback in vain. It "seemed that midnight had most surely arrived for the Cinderella team" (Whitney Martin, Associated Press).

> ## "Going around those bases in the ninth inning, I just couldn't believe what was happening to me. It felt as if I was actually living one of those middle-of-the-night dreams. You know, everything was hazy."
> —Bobby Thomson

Don Newcombe had given up only four scattered hits, but he had tired. Alvin Dark singled, an infield hit off first baseman Gil Hodges' glove. Don Mueller slashed a single right through where Hodges would have played had he not been holding Dark on the bag at first—unusual positioning given the three-run lead. Instead of a double play, there were two on and nobody out. Irvin fouled out, and the Dodgers had a respite and kept their three-run lead. Only two outs remained, but there were two Giants on base. Lockman doubled in one run, and now the Giants had men on second and third. A decent hit could tie the game. Hope was rekindled among the Polo Grounds fans.

Mueller had hurt his foot sliding into third and had to be removed. Red Smith wrote that it was the "corniest possible bit of Hollywood schmaltz—stretcher-bearers plodding away with an

Coming into the 1951 season, the Dodgers' Ralph Branca had 63 wins against 44 losses. When playing their cross-borough National League rivals, though, he was anything but a Giant killer in 1951.

Facing the New York Giants, Branca won just one game in 1951—on July 4. Six times that year he started against the Giants and six times the Giants won. Branca gave up 21 home runs in 1951: 11 of them were hit by the Giants, 10 by the other six teams combined.

Branca bore both Brooklyn playoff losses, both due to Bobby Thomson home runs. (Branca had also lost the first-ever playoff game in history, on October 1, 1946, to the St. Louis Cardinals.) Branca started the first game of the three-game playoff to determine the pennant, but he yielded two home runs, one to Monte Irvin and a two-run homer to Bobby Thomson, itself sufficient margin for Brooklyn's 3–1 defeat.

Maybe Charlie Dressen thought it was time for Branca's luck to turn around. Maybe he wasn't fazed by the disturbing fact that Branca wore No. 13 on the back of his uniform. With the exception of the Giants, Branca had a very good record in 1951. It's been suggested that the Giants were stealing signs that season, and that this petty larceny was responsible for their success against the Dodgers. It seems a feeble excuse. Sign stealing is a time-honored part of baseball, hardly industrial espionage. Whatever the reason, Thomson seemed to have Branca's number.

In some respects, Branca never recovered, although he did change his uniform number. The eight-year veteran pitcher won only 12 more major league games over the next four seasons.

Branca was so troubled, reported *The New York Times*' Ira Berkow, that at one point he asked a priest, "Father, why did this have to happen to me?" The priest replied, "God gave you this cross to bear because he knew you'd be strong enough to carry it."

In time, Branca became reconciled to his history. He continued to live in the New York area, becoming a successful insurance broker. Active in baseball alumni circles, he led the Baseball Assistance Team's efforts for years. Branca and Thomson have made several joint appearances at baseball memorabilia and card shows.

injured Mueller between them, symbolic of the Giants themselves." Manager Chuck Dressen brought in Ralph Branca to close out the game for Newcombe. Walking Thomson might have made sense. First base was open, and Thomson was hot. He already had two hits—a single and a double—and he had made that sacrifice fly back in the seventh. He also had 31 home runs on the season, fifth in the league.

Dressen may have been thinking of some recent history, too. In the 1947 World Series, the Yankees' Bucky Harris had ordered an

The shot! Bobby Thomson of the New York Giants hit one of the most famous home runs in baseball history, against the Brooklyn Dodgers at the Polo Grounds in New York City, October 3, 1951. The homer, hit during the last part of the ninth inning in the third and final playoff game, won not only the game but also the pennant.

intentional walk, only to see it come back and beat him in a 2–1 Yankees loss. And Dressen may have thought he'd be pressing his luck too much: already five times in 1951 he'd walked the potentially winning run, yet won every game. Did he fear he couldn't pull it off a sixth time?

Branca had pitched two innings on Sunday and eight more in Monday's playoff game. Now it was Wednesday and he was being called on again.

Given how hot Thomson had been, Giants manager Leo Durocher said he would have walked him, that he "never got a bigger or better surprise in my life" than when Dressen decided to pitch to the Staten Island Scot (so nicknamed because he was born in Glasgow, Scotland).

Thomson believed the pause in the action, prompted by Mueller's injury at third and the change of pitchers, helped calm him down and make him looser.

Branca's first pitch was a fastball right over the plate. Thomson took the pitch for strike one. The second was high and tight—a fastball—but not as inside as Branca had intended, and Thomson leaned back and hit it deep to left field, where it landed a very few feet into the stands, 315 feet away from home plate. The left-field corner was approximately 280 feet from home plate.

It was a home run that won the game—and the pennant—for the Giants, 5–4. The fat lady whipped off her Dodgers cap, replaced it with a Giants cap, and belted out her song.

After the game, Thomson said, "If I was a good hitter, I'd have taken that one. It was a bad pitch." Good enough for him, however, and for all Giants fans, whether in the crowd, listening on the radio, or watching on TV—the very first nationally televised game. What a debut!

All his teammates were waiting for Thomson as he crossed the plate—after making sure he touched every base. The only two Giants not in the group were manager Leo Durocher and second baseman Eddie Stanky, who were lying on the ground near third base. Durocher had become excitable and rushed toward the field, and Stanky tackled him to ensure that Thomson would indeed be able to make it around the bases without Durocher impeding his necessary circuit.

Staten Island now had "its greatest hometown hero since Giovanni de Verrazano discovered the island in 1524," as one journalist wrote. The Giants' comeback had won most baseball fans over, save those in Brooklyn. The *Boston Globe*'s Hy Hurwitz termed the Giants the "darlings of destiny and the peoples' choice." Destiny denied them the chance to beat the Yankees in the World Series, even though the Giants actually won two of the first three games. There were to be no more miracles for the Giants in 1951. But Bobby Thomson's playoff homer remains one of the touchstones of baseball history.

New York Giants players and fans converge on Thomson (with his head being rubbed) to reward him with a mauling after his pennant-winning, three-run home run. Running in to the left is Ed Stanky. Trying to get to Thomson is manager Leo Durocher (hatless, third from left).

2

The Greatest Game Ever Played

December 28, 1958, Yankee Stadium, the Bronx, New York

For millions of people around the country, the 1958 NFL championship game was their first exposure to professional football, brought into their living rooms through the magic of television. What a game the New York Giants and the Baltimore Colts gave them.

The Colts took a 14–3 halftime lead, only to see the Giants come back and move ahead, 17–14, in the fourth quarter, setting up a dramatic finish that produced the first sudden-death overtime in NFL history.

The Giants were threatening to run out the clock and win the championship. On third down and four, when a first down almost certainly would have meant a New York victory, Frank Gifford took the handoff from Charlie Conerly and headed toward the first-down marker.

Baltimore defensive end Gino Marchetti got to Gifford and brought him down, but in the pileup, Marchetti broke both his tibia and his fibula in his right leg. The officials waited for Marchetti to be carried off the field before marking the ball, and when they measured, the ball was five inches short of a first down.

"I saw him pick it [the ball] up at his front foot and put it down where his back foot was," New York receiver Kyle Rote said of the official. "He was too concerned about Marchetti."

Said Gifford, "I made that first down. I know I did."

According to the officials, however, it was fourth down, and, electing not to gamble and try again to get the first down, New York coach Jim Lee Howell sent in the punting team. A fair catch gave Baltimore possession at its own 14-yard line with 1:56 left in regulation.

"When we got in the huddle, I looked down the field," said Baltimore wide receiver Raymond Berry. "The goal posts looked like they were in Baltimore."

Quarterback Johnny Unitas elected to use the middle of the field, hoping he would have more room to find his receivers. He hit Lenny Moore for an 11-yard gain and then teamed up with Berry for completions of 25, 16, and 21 yards. Unitas had moved the Colts to the New York 13-yard line with seven seconds to

> ## "We all got our confidence from Johnny. I can't explain it but I absolutely knew we were going to score on that drive."
> —Colts receiver Raymond Berry

play. Kicker Steve Myhra made the field goal that sent the game into overtime.

New York won the coin toss and chose to receive. The Baltimore defense rose up, however, and stopped the Giants a yard short of first down, forcing another punt. The Colts took over on their own 20-yard line.

At least on this drive Unitas didn't have to worry about the clock stopping him, only the Giants defense. He decided to try to keep the ball on the ground as much as possible, minimizing the chances for a turnover.

Unitas moved the Colts to their own 43, but then went back to pass, only to be sacked for an eight-yard loss. That brought up third-and-15. Unitas called a play the Colts had put in specifically for this game but had yet to use. Moore lined up as the slot receiver, but when he was covered, Unitas was forced to look for a secondary receiver and found Berry breaking free from his defender. Unitas hit him for a 20-yard gain and a first down.

HALL OF FAME GAME

One of the reasons many people believe the 1958 NFL championship game between the Baltimore Colts and the New York Giants was the greatest game ever played is the assembly of talent that was on both sides of the ball. A total of 15 people who participated in the game as a coach or a player were later elected to the Pro Football Hall of Fame. Here is a look at their pro careers.

BALTIMORE
Coach

Weeb Ewbank—Only coach to win world championships in both NFL and AFL. Inducted in 1978.

Players

John Unitas—All-NFL 1957–1959, 1964–1965, 1967. Player of the Year three times. MVP three times in 10 Pro Bowls. Inducted in 1979.

Raymond Berry—All-NFL 1958–1960. Played in five Pro Bowl games. Inducted in 1973.

Jim Parker—First full-time offensive lineman named to the Hall of Fame. All-NFL eight straight years, 1958–1965. Inducted in 1973.

Lenny Moore—All-NFL 1958–1961, 1964. Played in seven Pro Bowls. Voted Comeback Player of Year in 1964. Inducted in 1975.

Gino Marchetti—Chosen for a record 11 straight Pro Bowls. Named All-NFL 1956–1964. Inducted in 1972.

Art Donovan—First Colt inducted to the Hall of Fame. All-NFL 1954–1957. Played in five Pro Bowls. Inducted in 1968.

NEW YORK
Assistant Coaches

Vince Lombardi—NFL Man of the Decade in the sixties. Led Packers to five NFL titles and two Super Bowl crowns in nine years. Inducted in 1971.

Tom Landry—Tied a record for 29 years with one team. Had 20 straight winning seasons, five NFC titles, and two Super Bowl wins. Inducted in 1990.

Players

Roosevelt Brown—All-NFL eight straight years, 1956–1963. Played in nine Pro Bowl games. Voted NFL's Lineman of Year in 1956. Inducted in 1975.

Frank Gifford—All-NFL 1955–1957, 1959. NFL Player of Year in 1956. Inducted in 1977.

Andy Robustelli—Played in eight NFL title games and seven Pro Bowls. Recovered 22 career fumbles. Missed only one game in 14 years. Inducted in 1971.

Sam Huff—Played in six NFL title games and five Pro Bowls. Had 30 career interceptions. Inducted in 1982.

Don Maynard—Had more than 50 catches for 1,000 receiving yards in five different years. Played in three AFL All-Star games. Inducted in 1987.

Emlen Tunnell—Played in nine Pro Bowls. All-NFL 1951–1952, 1954–1957. Inducted in 1967.

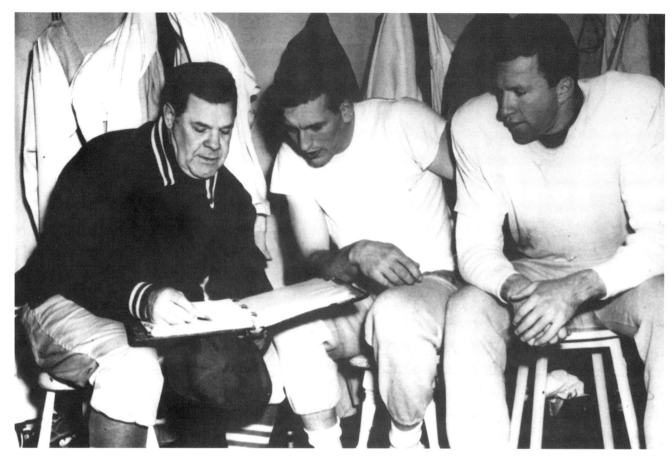

Baltimore Colts head coach Weeb Ewbank goes over a game plan with quarterbacks Johnny Unitas (center) and George Shaw.

Baltimore Colts fullback Alan Ameche advances through a big opening provided by teammates to score the winning touchdown in overtime. The Colts' Lenny Moore got a good block on the Giants' Emlen Tunnell (No. 45, at left). Unitas (No. 19, at right) ran right along with the Giants' Jim Patton (No. 20).

Unitas had noticed how aggressively the Giants defensive line was playing, and so he called for a handoff that was designed to take advantage of the situation.

"We figured that [Dick] Modzelewski would come flying through there," Unitas said. "He did and everything worked out the way it was supposed to—[Alan] Ameche went clean up the middle."

The play resulted in a 23-yard gain by Ameche that moved the ball to the Giants' 20. One play later, Unitas and Berry teamed up for a 10-yard completion.

Despite the fact that the Colts were in definite field-goal range, they kept pushing for a touchdown. Unitas called for a dangerous pass play across the field that easily could have been intercepted. Instead, Jim Mutscheller hauled it in and took it to the 1-yard line.

From there Ameche powered into the end zone, and Baltimore began celebrating its NFL championship.

Unitas, who had come back into the Colts lineup after suffering cracked ribs and a punctured lung in midseason, had followed his last-minute drive of 86 yards in the fourth quarter to tie the game with an 80-yard, 13-play drive in overtime for the victory. He finished the day completing 26 of 40 passes for 349 yards. Twelve of his completions went to Berry for 178 yards.

"When you allow a club to go all the way twice as the Colts did to tie the game at 17 and then to win it in the extra period, then you can only say they are great," Howell said. "We have a very fine defense and the Colts went through it. We couldn't contain them on the big plays in the crucial spots."

Ewbank briefs his team for the 1958 NFL championship game against the New York Giants.

3

Miracle on Ice

February 22, 1980, Olympic Field House, Lake Placid, New York

Never yet in these Olympic Games had the U.S. hockey team faced such a daunting task. True, the Americans had come back before in the tournament. Against high-powered Czechoslovakia in the second game of the round-robin stage, the Yanks climbed out of an early 1–0 deficit to demolish the more experienced Europeans, 7–2. Later, they did the same against West Germany, netting four unanswered goals to erase a 2–0 deficit and notch their fourth win of the Olympics.

Now, however, in the semifinal at Lake Placid's Olympic Field House, the Americans trailed the formidable Soviet Union, winners of five of the previous six Olympic hockey gold medals. This was a Soviet squad renowned for its conditioning and skill, a team many believed to be the equal of any in the National Hockey League. In a pre-Olympic exhibition game at Madison Square Garden, the Russians had humbled Team USA by a score of 10–3. So when the Americans found themselves trailing, 3–2, heading into the third and final period of the Olympic semifinal, few thought this group of college kids and recent NHL draft picks had the wherewithal to stay with the Russians, much less turn the game around.

Throughout the tournament, coach Herb Brooks had taken full advantage of his team's youthfulness, telling his players to "use your enthusiasm." Now that youth, in the form of inexperience, could work against them, and all the enthusiasm in the world wouldn't be enough.

The Russians had jumped out to an early lead when their own young star, Valery Krotov, deflected a slap shot from Alexei Kasatonov past American goaltender Jim Craig. The Americans didn't back down, though, as 25-year-old William "Buzz" Schneider went high on Russian goalie Vladislav Tretiak to score his team-leading fifth goal of the Olympics and tie the game at one apiece.

Late in the first period, however, the Russians pulled ahead on a goal by Sergei Makarov. The hosts complained that referee Karl-Gustav Kaisla had failed to notice an American player being held when Makarov took his shot. Still, the Yanks wouldn't quit.

> "I don't think you can put it into words. It was 20 guys pulling for each other, never quitting, 60 minutes of good hockey. It's a human emotion that is indescribable."
>
> —U.S. Olympic hockey team captain Mike Eruzione

With only seconds left in the period, New York Islanders draftee Ken Marrow fired an 80-foot slap shot toward the Russian net. The puck rebounded off Tretiak and found its way to center Mark Johnson, 22, the hottest prospect on the American squad. Johnson poked the puck past the Soviet netminder, but when he turned to look at the scoreboard, the clock showed zeros. Was it a goal or not? According to hockey rules, the puck must cross the goal line before time expires. Kaisla eventually ruled that it had crossed the line in time, inciting fury in the Russians and a roar of approval from the red-white-and-blue crowd.

The second period saw the Russians pull a goalie switch, as Vladimir Myshkin took over for Tretiak in net. The change paid off, as Myshkin stopped both shots sent his way in the period. On the other end, Craig was under constant attack as the Soviets played their fluid, deadly attacking game around the embattled netminder. Despite Craig's best efforts, the Russians

TEAM USA

When the young Americans pulled ahead, 3–2, in the third and final period, few thought this collection of kids (their average age was 22) could pull off the upset—except coach Herb Brooks and his team. But the coach knew the power of youth, telling his team, "use your enthusiasm." And they did. Below is the roster of the young Olympic heroes, with their tender ages and the colleges and universities where they learned to play the game.

- Steven Janaszak, 23, University of Minnesota
- James Craig, 23, Boston University
- Kenneth Morrow, 22, Bowling Green
- Michael Ramsey, 18, University of Minnesota
- William Baker, 22, University of Minnesota
- John O'Callahan, 21, Boston University
- Bob Suter, 22, University of Wisconsin
- David Silk, 21, Boston University
- Neal Broten, 19, University of Minnesota
- Mark Johnson, 22, University of Wisconsin
- Steven Christoff, 21, Boston University
- Mark Wells, 21, Bowling Green
- Mark Pavelich, 21, Minnesota–Duluth
- Eric Strobel, 21, University of Minnesota
- Michael Eruzione, 25, Boston University
- David Christian, 20, University of North Dakota
- Robert McLanahan, 21, University of Minnesota
- William "Buzz" Schneider, 24, University of Minnesota
- Philip Verchota, 22, University of Minnesota
- John Harrington, 22, Minnesota–Duluth

pulled ahead when veteran Aleksandr Maltsev scored on a power play. The Americans could get no attack going against a swift, aggressive Soviet defense. It appeared that their Cinderella run was finally coming to an end.

Of course, appearances can be deceiving. Inexperience notwithstanding, the United States had already displayed an uncanny ability to come back in the tournament, and in the third period the young Americans came out with their sights set on the victory that would propel them into the gold-medal match. Near the halfway mark of the third period, Johnson struck again, redirecting a shot by David Silk past Myshkin to tie the score. Team USA was back in the game, but they would need another hero to pull off one of the most shocking upsets in sports history.

Up stepped team captain Mike Eruzione, Craig's former teammate at Boston University. With 10 minutes remaining, Eruzione gained the puck in the Soviet zone and moved it toward Myshkin unimpeded. He then cocked and fired a 30-footer that Myshkin did not see leave the stick. The puck found space between the Russian goaltender's bulky pads and kissed the back of the net.

The Field House crowd erupted into wild cheers and rafter-rattling chants of "U-S-A, U-S-A!" that would only grow more intense as the period wound down. When the final buzzer sounded pandemonium broke loose, both in the stands and on the ice. The American players threw their equipment into the air and embraced in wonder at their achievement. Draped in the Stars and Stripes, Craig, one of

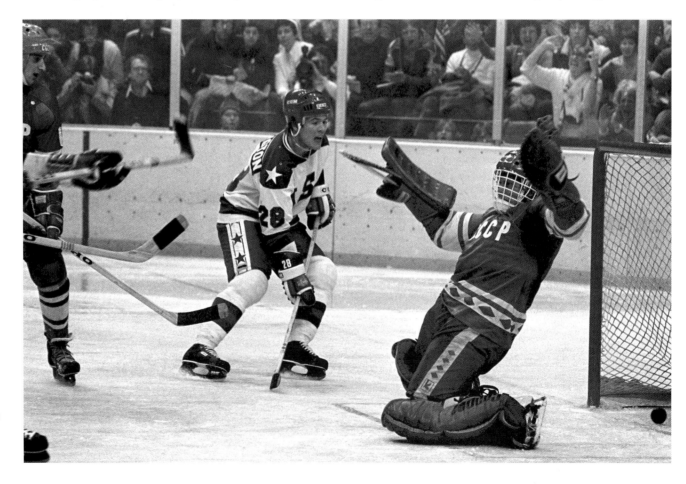

As American John Harrington looks on, the puck slips past Soviet goaltender Vladimir Myshkin with 10 minutes remaining in the third period of the 1980 Olympic hockey semifinal. The goal snapped a 3–3 tie. The game winner came from the stick of U.S. captain Mike Eruzione (not pictured).

the true heroes of the game, sought out his family in the stands. Although the match was not broadcast live on television, news of the tremendous upset spread like wildfire across the country. When the final score was announced at Radio City Music Hall in New York City, the crowd cheered and began an impromptu singing of the national anthem. All over the nation, Americans embraced in bars and living rooms as the shocking final score flashed across their television screens. "I'm sure the 20 guys won't believe it," said Johnson of his victorious teammates. "They'll probably wake up tomorrow morning and still won't believe it."

The quest for gold was not over, of course. There was still Finland in the final. But after the miraculous victory over the Soviet powerhouse, that match was all but a formality, as the United States won 4–2 to earn hockey gold for the first time since the equally stunning victory in Squaw Valley 20 years earlier. In 1980, America embraced its young heroes as it had no hockey players before. For one glorious moment, the Cold War was won and the United States could boast of having the best hockey team in the world.

Coach Herb Brooks and his bench (above) remained stoic through the final 10 minutes of the 1980 Olympic hockey semifinal, while their team protected a 4–3 lead.

Team USA is still getting honors today: here they are wildly cheered before lighting the Olympic torch during the opening ceremonies at the 2002 Winter Games in Salt Lake City. Eruzione (center) scored the game-winning goal.

4

Jordan's Parting Shot

June 14, 1998, Delta Center, Salt Lake City, Utah

The Chicago Bulls have demonstrated an uncanny ability to produce magic on the court time and again. The fiercely loyal fans of the 1998 Bulls knew that stars Michael Jordan, Scottie Pippen, and coach Phil Jackson combined to create an almost mythical force that would never come their way again. Although the trio ultimately broke up after the season, they would go out with a bang.

Chicago won the NBA title in 1996 and 1997, but could it happen again in 1998? This season the team was making a run for the three-peat. That may sound impressive—maybe even impossible—for anyone but the Bulls in the nineties. This was a team who knew their goals were attainable. After all, they had pulled off the same feat in 1991, 1992, and 1993.

This series of playoffs, in fact, was strangely reminiscent of the 1993 title run. In 1993 the Bulls were leading the Phoenix Suns three games to one. With the arrogance of a city that is used to seeing its team win, Chicago television stations ran public service announcements warning fans to celebrate sensibly. Downtown businesses nailed plywood over their glass windows. But the Bulls lost Game 5, sending the finals back down to Phoenix.

Five years later the Bulls once again had a 3–1 series lead, this time over the Utah Jazz. Game 5 was in Chicago, with fans planning their victory parties. The Bulls played hard, but it wasn't enough. An 83–81 loss to the Jazz sent the teams back to Utah and the Delta Center for Game 6.

"I think this is the toughest game to win," Pippen said of the series clincher. "It's going to be very hard."

Jordan agreed. "It's not easy walking into Utah and trying to win," he said. "I welcome the challenge."

Misfortune struck the Bulls early when Pippen, who had injured his back in a previous game, reinjured it at the start of Game 6. A cortisone shot bought him a little relief, but it was short-lived. He was only able to play seven minutes in the first half, scoring just eight points.

Emotions ran high at the Delta Center as the Jazz ran into troubles of their own. They were frustrated by two 24-second violations that ultimately wiped out five points. Television replays later showed that there was actually one-tenth of a second left on the clock when Howard Eisley sunk a three-

> # "The moment started to come, and once you get the moment, you see the court and you see what the defense wants to do. I saw that moment."
> ## —Michael Jordan

pointer. "We have no control over that," said coach Jerry Sloan. "That's part of the business."

Poor shooting by both teams left the game up for grabs early on. But who had the best defense? In the two games won by Utah, they were able to contain Jordan, forcing him to take poor shots and make bad passes. But as always, Michael Jordan proved to be a challenge, demonstrating why he had won the NBA scoring title each of his 10 full seasons on the court.

The teams were evenly matched for the first half, with shots alternating back and forth. An offensive rebound by Karl Malone led to a six-foot jumper and a 39–36 lead for the Jazz. Jordan hit a three-pointer from the right wing, but Malone answered with a shot from the baseline. Toni Kukoc and Bryon Russell each scored before Jordan let loose a 17-footer to tie the game at 45. Finally, two Utah layups gave them the 49–45 lead at halftime.

THE END OF A BULLS DYNASTY

Even as the Bulls won their third NBA title in three years and their sixth in eight years, an era was coming to an end.

Michael Jordan, voted Finals MVP for a record sixth time in 1998, made his desires clear. He wanted to make a run for one more championship—but only if teammate Scottie Pippen and coach Phil Jackson could be part of the package.

As the players and Bulls management gathered at center court to claim the title, owner Jerry Reinsdorf made nice for the media. "I can only hope and pray that Michael and Scottie will come back and defend the championship one more time," he said. Unfortunately, behind closed doors Reinsdorf and general manager Jerry Krause appeared to have other ideas.

Public opinion of the pair was at an all-time low among loyal Bulls fans, who resented any tampering with the status quo, especially after Chicago walked away with another NBA title. If the Bulls had failed in their attempt at a three-peat, Reinsdorf may have had reason to make personnel changes, but their number one finish raised questions as to why management would fix what wasn't broken. "There are a lot of sympathetic feelings about this team and where we want it to go," said Jordan.

"You hate to see it come to an end," agreed Pippen. "It's been a lot of fun." But it finally came down to finances for Pippen, who was insulted that the Bulls were unwilling to sweeten his deal, leaving the free agent only the 122nd highest paid player in the league. His bid for a three-year contract worth $45 million didn't seem likely to be endorsed by the money-conscious Reinsdorf.

To complicate matters, Krause had already given coach Phil Jackson his walking papers before the game. After cleaning out his desk at the United Center, Jackson gave voice to what most people already guessed. "I don't expect to see us back here again," he said.

Ultimately, even the game-winning heroics of Michael Jordan were not enough to keep the team intact. The 35-year-old out of North Carolina finished his 14th year with his 10th scoring championship, an unparalleled 10th all-NBA team berth, his 9th all-defensive first team spot, and his 5th league MVP award.

And of course, he'll never forget the memories of one last magical game played—and won—with his friends and teammates, the 1998 Chicago Bulls. As Jackson said of that last season together, "How sweet it is."

Michael Jordan holds up six fingers for the six NBA Championships the Chicago Bulls dynasty of the nineties had won.

Pippen returned at the beginning of the third quarter. "I was hurting pretty bad," he said, "but I thought my presence on the floor would mean more than just sitting in the locker room."

Even with the pain, he managed to come up with three rebounds, four assists, and two steals by the end of the game. Most of the scoring would be left to his teammates, however.

With just over six minutes left in the third quarter, Karl Malone and the Bulls' Dennis Rodman engaged in a physical matchup that led to a Rodman foul. Malone promptly sank one of his two free throws, giving the Jazz a 54–51 lead.

The momentum turned and the Jazz increased their lead to 66–61 by the start of the fourth quarter. With 12 minutes on the clock, it looked as though Game 7 was going to become a reality.

Utah was up by as many as eight points in the final quarter when Jordan turned on the heat. He had 16 points, including eight free throws, a rebound, and two steals in the last 12 minutes. A jumper by Malone put Utah ahead, 83–79, with two and a half minutes remaining.

The rest was all Jordan.

He scored the Bulls' final eight points of the game, pulling within one with 37 seconds on the clock. Holding onto a one-point lead, the Jazz ran some time off the clock before going inside to Malone, who was covered by Rodman. Jordan slipped in behind Malone, stripping the ball away with 18.9 seconds left. In typical Jordan style, the MVP hit a 17-footer with 5.2 seconds on the clock.

Utah called one last timeout to set up a three-point attempt by John Stockton. The shot missed, and the Bulls picked up their third NBA title in as many years.

With a total of 45 points, it's no wonder that coach Phil Jackson gave credit to Jordan. "He does it again and again in the clutch," said Jackson. "I think it's the best Michael Jordan moment ever."

Speculation ran high as to whether Jordan and his buddies would be back for another year, but Jordan took the victory and the future in stride. "Hopefully I've put enough memories out there in my 14 years," he said.

Series MVP Jordan is doused with champagne by teammate Pippen (right) while holding the NBA championship trophy.

5

The Ice Bowl

December 31, 1967, Lambeau Field, Green Bay, Wisconsin

To say this Sunday in late December dawned clear and cold would have been a gross understatement. The 1967 NFL championship was on the line, and the Green Bay Packers and Dallas Cowboys had winning—not weather—on their minds.

But Mother Nature was already at work. The mercury plunged to a record-setting 13 degrees below zero, and a wind chill of 48 below zero made the air feel more like Alaska than Green Bay, Wisconsin. It's no wonder that this New Year's Eve game would go down in history as the "Ice Bowl."

Until close to game time, Packers coach Vince Lombardi would have sworn up and down that tough guys don't worry about the weather. In fact, Lombardi had done all he could to make sure they wouldn't have to; the previous season he had an $80,000 heating system installed the length of the field to ensure that the surface would be in optimum playing condition in any weather. Possibly the heating coils did their job too well. Unfortunately, the warm air created condensation between the field and the tarp. When the tarp was lifted, the arctic air hit the field and turned it into an ice rink.

"It was like being at the North Pole," said Cowboys coach Tom Landry of the intense cold. NFL commissioner Pete Rozelle checked with team physicians before deciding that the game should go on, and officials were forced to shout plays dead after referee Norm Schachter's whistle froze to his lip. But if excitement alone could warm the stadium, the 50,861 fans would have been taking off their shirts.

As the game began, the Packers had the advantage of home (albeit frozen) turf, but the Cowboys were riding high after a 52–14 win over the Cleveland Browns the week before. They had high hopes of winning their first NFL title and ending the Packers' bid to be the first team in league history to win three consecutive championships.

At first, history appeared to be repeating itself. Just as they had done a year before in the 1966 championship game, Green Bay jumped to an early 14–0 lead. By the second quarter, however, the Cowboys were adjusting to the bitter cold and coming up with some big plays of their own.

> ## "We were ready on that last drive. We were totally focused on what we needed to do in order to go down and win. As I looked into the eyes of my teammates, I knew all I had to do was call the play."
> —Packers quarterback Bart Starr

Two Packers fumbles were all it took for the momentum to change. The temperature was colder than ever, but by halftime the game was suddenly heating up, and the score was a close 14–10.

The locker room focus was on thawing out, with a few choice words by the coaches designed to spur the players on to victory. "We thought we were still in charge," said Packers fullback Chuck Mercein, "but we knew we still had football to play and that it was time to hunker down."

The Cowboys, it seemed, were of the same opinion, and they came out psyched to win. The Packers were set to receive at the start of the second half, but the Cowboys squelched their momentum by stuffing a Donny Anderson run, sacking Bart Starr, and blocking a pass intended for receiver Boyd Dowler. After a scoreless third quarter, Dallas turned up the juice once again with a touchdown eight seconds into the fourth quarter

BY THE NUMBERS: HOW THE GAME PLAYED OUT

	1st	2nd	3rd	4th	Total
Dallas	0	10	0	7	17
Green Bay	7	7	0	7	21

Green Bay—Dowler 8 pass from Starr (Chandler kick)
Green Bay—Dowler 43 pass from Starr (Chandler kick)
Dallas—Andrie 7 return of Starr fumble (Villanueva kick)
Dallas—Rentzel 50 pass from Reeves (Villanueva kick)
Green Bay—Starr 1 run (Chandler kick)

STATISTICS
Rushing
Dallas—Perkins, 17 for 51; Reeves, 13 for 42; Meredith, 1 for 9; Baynham, 1 for -2; Clarke, 1 for -8

Green Bay—Anderson, 18 for 35; Mercein, 6 for 20; Williams, 4 for 13; Wilson, 3 for 11; Starr, 1 for 1, 1 TD

Passing
Dallas—Meredith, 10 of 25 for 59; Reeves, 1 of 1 for 50, 1 TD

Green Bay—Starr, 14 of 24 for 191, 2 TDs

Receiving
Dallas—Rentzel, 2 for 61, 1 TD; Clarke, 2 for 24; Hayes, 3 for 16; Reeves, 3 for 11; Baynham, 1 for -3

Green Bay—Dowler, 4 for 77, 2 TDs; Anderson, 4 for 44; Dale, 3 for 44; Mercein, 2 for 22; Williams, 1 for 4

Team Statistics	Dallas	Green Bay
First downs	11	18
Rushing	4	5
Passing	6	10
By penalty	1	3
Total yardage	192	195
Net rushing yards	92	80
Net passing yards	100	115
Passes attempted	26	24
Passes completed	11	14
Interceptions	1	0

Attendance: 50,861

AN ALL-STARR QUARTERBACK

Sports fans are a crazy bunch. When a player is winning, he's a god; when he's losing, he's worse than pond scum. In Green Bay in the sixties, Bart Starr was a god. By the time he retired, he could have been elected president.

But Bart Starr was an unlikely hero. Joe Namath he was not. In fact, his nondescript appearance brought him little attention walking down the street. He was of medium build with brownish hair, a receding hairline, and small eyes. His 6'1", 200-pound frame was athletic, but not exceptional.

Born Bryan Bartlett Starr in Dadeville, Alabama, Bart learned to play football from his father. He went on to play at the University of Alabama, although his college career was not as special as you would imagine. In fact, he barely played, even as a senior.

Continued on page 21

Dallas Cowboys defensive end George Andrie picks up a Bart Starr fumble, ready to follow teammate Jethro Pugh (No. 75) into the end zone to score.

on a 50-yard pass from halfback Dan Reeves to Lance Rentzel. The Cowboys were riding high with a 17–14 lead.

The home team went 37:15 without scoring before they finally gained a little momentum of their own.

There was 5:04 remaining on the clock when the Packers got the ball on their own 32-yard line. "We were ready on that last drive," said Starr. "We were totally focused on what we needed to do in order to go down and win. As I looked into the eyes of my teammates, I knew that all I had to do was call the play."

And play calling was what the former University of Alabama quarterback was known for. Teammate Jerry Kramer said, "Bart was

rarely the best quarterback in the league on a statistical basis. But for three hours each Sunday, he was almost always the best quarterback in the game." And this frigid Sunday in December was no different.

With just 68 yards between the Packers and an unprecedented third championship, Bart Starr began the most famous drive of his career.

Green Bay moved the chains 38 yards as the crowd watched three minutes tick off the clock. A 19-yard pass to Mercein finally stopped the clock and earned the Packers a first down.

With 11 yards to go, Starr called what he now considers to be the best call of his life—a "give" or "sucker" play. When guard Gale Gillingham faked to his right, Dallas tackle Bob Lilly followed, opening a hole for Mercein, who dove to the 3-yard line. Less than a minute remained on the clock.

Starr then handed off to Donny Anderson, who plunged another two yards for a Green Bay first down at the 1-yard line. On second down, Anderson was stopped at the line of scrimmage on the same play.

The Packers called a timeout with 20 seconds on the clock. By now the wind chill had dipped to an unbelievable 50 below. The frozen tundra that was Lambeau Field made play next to impossible, but hoping the third time would be a charm, Starr once again handed off to Anderson. The running back slipped on the icy turf, stopping a mere foot short of the goal line, and Green Bay took their final timeout.

With 16 seconds on the scoreboard the sellout crowd stomped their numb toes and screamed for the home team, but the Pack was still on the short end of the 17–14 score.

There are several schools of thought on what the Packers should have done. A field goal would tie the game, sending the teams into overtime. A pass was another option; if it didn't work, Green Bay could still run, pass, or kick on fourth down. But Starr had other ideas. He wanted to go for the victory.

Handing off was a risk on the icy field, so Starr made his case in the sideline conference to go for a quarterback sneak. Lombardi agreed, saying, "Then let's run it and get the hell out of here."

Starr returned to the huddle, calling for a 31 wedge. That was the signal for Jerry Kramer and Kenny Bowman to double-team defensive tackle Jethro Pugh, opening a small hole for Starr, who was ready. He lunged into the end zone—and the record books.

The extra point was good and the Packers took the lead with 13 seconds remaining. Two incomplete passes by the Cowboys ran out the clock to give Green Bay the come-from-behind, 21–17 win and their third consecutive championship.

Years later Cowboys coach Tom Landry would remember that day. "I can't believe that call, the sneak," he said. "It wasn't a good call. But now it's a great call."

Continued from page 19

Still dreaming of a pro career, Starr was drafted by the last-place Packers in the 17th round of the football draft. Even then, he was almost cut from the roster. Packers coaches were skeptical that he could do the job, and he found himself riding the bench his first few years in Green Bay.

The truth is, Starr didn't have the raw talent, the athleticism, of many quarterbacks. He wasn't Brett Favre. But he was smarter than many of his peers. Thinking through the plays, analyzing the way the defense was lined up, and changing audibles were his greatest strengths.

His gifts served him well in 1967, the final game of the year. The last play would go down in history as the greatest moment in football. Starr's quarterback sneak won the game for Green Bay, sending his team into the Super Bowl.

Starr's number was retired in 1973, he accepted the Packers head coaching job in 1975, and he was inducted into the Pro Football Hall of Fame in 1977. Not bad for a 17th-round draft pick.

Starr (No. 15, at left foreground) digs his face across the goal line to score the winning touchdown and bring the Packers their third consecutive NFL championship.

6

The Immaculate Reception

All Franco Harris did was react. He saw the football coming toward him, reached toward the ground, and caught it just off the tops of his shoes, then he took off for the end zone.

Little did Harris realize that he was running into football history, completing a play that is still known today as the "Immaculate Reception," which lifted the Pittsburgh Steelers to a 13–7 playoff victory over the Oakland Raiders.

Because of confusion over whether Oakland defensive back Jack Tatum had touched the ball after it hit Pittsburgh's John "Frenchy" Fuqua, the NFL supervisor of officials sitting in the press box at Three Rivers Stadium in Pittsburgh viewed televised replays of the play before conferring with the officials on the field. This marked the first time that instant replay was used to make certain that a call on the field was correct.

The ruling, both on the field by referee Fred Swearingen and his crew and from NFL official Art McNally in the press box, was that Tatum had touched the ball, making it a legally completed pass and a 60-yard touchdown. Under NFL rules at the time, changed in 1978, an offensive player was not allowed to deflect a ball to his teammate unless it was also touched by a defensive player.

The miracle pass came on a fourth down and 10 from Pittsburgh's 40-yard line as time was running out in the game. Oakland had gone ahead, 7–6, a minute earlier on a 30-yard touchdown run by quarterback Ken Stabler. Stabler had replaced starter Darryl Lamonica, who was suffering from the flu.

Taking over at his own 25 with 1:13 to play, Pittsburgh quarterback Terry Bradshaw completed two passes to move the ball to the 40. The drive stalled, however, as Bradshaw threw consecutive incompletions, two of the passes broken up by Tatum.

Bradshaw now faced a fourth-and-10 as he attempted to move the Steelers into position for a possible game-winning field goal. Only 20 seconds remained as he dropped back to pass and was chased out of the pocket by defensive end Tony Cline.

> ## "No one knows all the details. I don't know about Frenchy's part. He doesn't know about my part. It makes it kind of interesting that way."
> —Steelers running back Franco Harris

The play was designed to go to Barry Pearson, but he was covered.

As Bradshaw scrambled away from Cline, he spotted Fuqua downfield, who looked as if he was breaking open at the Oakland 35-yard line. The pass from Bradshaw arrived at Fuqua at the same time as Tatum.

As the ball bounced off the receiver, or Tatum, or both, it bounded a few yards toward Franco Harris, who had been blocking in the backfield but had gone downfield when he saw Bradshaw begin to scramble out of the pocket.

"If he threw to Frenchy, I thought I might get there in time to block for him," Harris said. "Just as I put it in gear, I saw the ball bounce off them and I said to myself, 'Oh no, it's all over.' Then I saw that it was bouncing toward me, and I felt I might get it if I kept going. I did."

Harris caught the ball and continued running. As soon as he crossed the goal line, with five seconds left in the game, the

THE IMMACULATE RECEPTION

Terry Bradshaw was selected as the first overall pick in the 1970 NFL draft by the Pittsburgh Steelers after they won a coin flip with the Chicago Bears, enabling them to make the top selection. It was a great deal for Pittsburgh, who ended up with one of the most prolific quarterbacks in NFL history. A fierce competitor who often called his own plays, Bradshaw was known for his excellent throwing arm and was at his best in big games. He was the only QB to lead his team to four Super Bowl victories. Bradshaw set numerous Super Bowl passing records and won two Super Bowl MVP Awards on his way to becoming a Hall of Fame quarterback. Bradshaw played 14 years in his career, all with the Steelers.

CAREER STATISTICS

Year	G	Passing Att.	Com.	%	Yds.	TD	Int.	Rtg.	Rushing Att.	Yds.	TD
1970	13	218	83	38.1	1,410	6	24	30.4	32	233	1
1971	14	373	203	54.4	2,259	13	22	59.7	53	247	5
1972	14	308	147	47.7	1,887	12	12	64.1	58	346	7
1973	10	180	89	49.4	1,183	10	15	54.5	34	145	3
1974	8	148	67	45.3	785	7	8	55.2	34	224	2
1975	14	286	165	57.7	2,055	18	9	88.0	35	210	3
1976	10	192	92	47.9	1,177	10	9	65.4	31	219	3
1977	14	314	162	51.6	2,523	17	19	71.4	31	171	3
1978	16	368	207	56.3	2,915	28	20	84.7	32	93	1
1979	16	472	259	54.9	3,724	26	25	77.0	21	83	0
1980	15	424	218	51.4	3,339	24	22	75.0	36	111	2
1981	14	370	201	54.3	2,887	22	14	83.9	38	162	2
1982	9	240	127	52.9	1,768	17	11	81.4	8	10	0
1983	1	8	5	62.5	77	20	13	3.9	1	3	0
Totals	168	3,901	2,025	51.7	27,989	230	223	70.9	444	2,257	32
Playoffs	19	456	261	57.2	3,833	30	26	83.0	52	274	3

G = game; Att. = attempts; Com. = completions; Yds. = yards; TD = touchdowns; Int. = interceptions; Rtg. = rating

Franco Harris (No. 32) eludes a tackle by Jimmy Warren of the Oakland Raiders on a 42-yard catch and run to score the winning touchdown in the American Conference playoff game in Pittsburgh on Sunday, December 23, 1972. Harris' "Immaculate Reception" came when a desperation pass to a teammate bounced off a Raiders defender. The touchdown gave Pittsburgh a 13–7 lead with five seconds left in the game.

controversy began. As the officials convened on the field, nobody knew if the touchdown would be allowed to stand or if it would be declared an incomplete pass.

"He really gave me a lick," Fuqua said of Tatum. "He dazed me. I hadn't seen him coming. I thought I had the ball, and just then I had the accident."

Tatum insisted he hit Fuqua but not the ball and that it should have been called an incomplete pass and Oakland declared the winner.

"I was covering the tight end when this dude cut in front of me," Tatum said. "I didn't know it was Fuqua. At first I thought I had a chance for the ball, but I didn't. Then I went for the man. I never did hit the ball."

Oakland coach John Madden agreed with his player. Madden saw the meeting of the officials and the delayed call as a sign that they were unsure what had happened, "or they would have made the call right away."

What viewers on television saw, and what the NFL official in the press box saw, was not conclusive. That left the call up to the judgment of the officials on the field, since there was no glaring evidence to indicate that Tatum had or had not touched the ball.

All of the controversy might never have developed had Pittsburgh coach Chuck Noll decided to kick a field goal in the scoreless first half on a fourth down and less than a yard from the Oakland 31. Instead, he decided to try for the first down, but Fuqua's run up the middle was stopped short.

Nobody knew at that moment the dramatic conclusion of the game that was to come.

Harris: the *most* immaculate receiver of all time.

The mainstays in the 1972 Steelers backfield (from left): Harris, quarterback Terry Bradshaw, and John "Frenchy" Fuqua.

7

Maz Makes History

October 13, 1960, Forbes Field, Pittsburgh

The 1960 World Series was unlike any October classic before or since. Some observers of the day characterized it as David versus Goliath or King Kong versus mere mortals; others drew parallels to the offensive mismatch at the Alamo. Still others were reminded of that classic Warner Brothers cartoon featuring Spike, the fearsome old bulldog, and his hyper little companion, Chester, a much less formidable breed who was looking for respect. Spike was the 1960 American League champion New York Yankees, and that pip-squeak pup was the 1960 National League champion Pittsburgh Pirates.

Just how big a mismatch was this World Series? On paper it was huge. On paper, the 1960 Yankees led the American League in virtually every significant offensive category. They scored 746 runs, crushed 193 home runs, and compiled a .426 slugging percentage. Not to be outdone, their pitchers led the junior circuit in ERA (3.52), saves (42), and shutouts (16). The Yanks boasted the M&M boys, Mickey Mantle and Roger Maris, who finished one-two in the home-run derby with 40 and 39, respectively. Their supporting cast would have been headliners on any other team. In fact, including manager Casey Stengel, the Yankees had no fewer than four future Hall of Famers in uniform that season. The others were Mantle, Whitey Ford, and Yogi Berra. The Pirates also had a couple of future Hall of Famers in Roberto Clemente and Bill Mazeroski, but Clemente had yet to hit his offensive stride, and the scouting reports indicated that Maz was strictly a glove man. On paper there was no way the Pirates could scuttle the Bronx Bombers.

How lopsided were the wins? After the Pirates' narrow 6–4 victory in Game 1 (Mazeroski's two-run homer had carried the day), the Yankees took out their frustrations at the plate in Game 2, pounding out 19 hits and plating 16 runs in a 16–3 pummeling. With future Hall of Famer Whitey Ford toeing the rubber in Game 3 at Yankee Stadium, the Yankees continued the onslaught, plundering the Pirates, 10–0, on the strength of 16 hits. The Yankees were now up two games to one, and it looked like a rout.

The Jekyll and Hyde series continued in Game 4, as starter Vernon Law and reliever Roy Face held the mighty Bronx Bombers to just two runs, earning the Pirates a 3–2 win and evening the Series, 2–2. In Game 5, Pirates second baseman Bill Mazeroski again proved to be the hero of the day as he doubled in two runs and led the National League champs past the Yanks

"Every day of my life I think of that home run. I suppose it might have been the most important thing I've ever done."
—Pirates second baseman Bill Mazeroski

by a three-run margin, the final score 5–2. Unbelievably, the Pittsburgh Pirates were up three games to two and on the verge of winning the Series. But as the Series moved back to Steel Town for Game 6, the real Yankees showed up once more and again it was a slaughter. The Yankees scored 12 runs and distributed 17 hits all over Forbes Field.

It would all come down to the final game. Game 7 had it all. Weird plays, home runs, comebacks, more comebacks, and a final comeback—drama of the highest order. It was as if Abner Doubleday wanted to show off his sport and decided to condense every aspect of the game into first seven games, then nine innings, and ultimately a single ninth inning.

Game 7 was another slugfest, and on paper that seemed to be good news for the Yankees. They were, after all, the ones with the

When Bucs second baseman Bill Mazeroski was finally elected to the Hall of Fame in 2001, many people felt the honor was long overdue. There appears to be a double standard in Cooperstown that favors hitters over fielders, but try to find a pitcher who doesn't value defense. If Maz had not gotten the baseball world's attention with one big swing of his bat, they may well have continued to ignore his accomplishments with the glove.

Yet Mazeroski set a new standard for second basemen by turning 1,706 double plays. He topped the National League in DPs eight times and in assists nine times. He also led in putouts five times and fielding average on three occasions. He captured eight Gold Gloves during his career. This was no average fielder. Baseball gurus John Thorn and Pete Palmer, writing in baseball's statistical bible *Total Baseball*, termed Mazeroski "possibly the greatest-fielding second baseman who ever lived."

The fact that he played on the same team and shared the DP credits with erratic first baseman Dick "Dr. Strangeglove" Stuart must surely be one of the great ironies of baseball. The only nonbaseball comparison that comes to mind is of Luciano Pavarotti and Placido Domingo being joined onstage by sixties-era novelty singer Tiny Tim. Stuart once even received a standing ovation from Pittsburgh's Forbes Field faithful by successfully scooping up a gum wrapper that had blown across the field. When the usual announcement was made before a home game, "Anyone who interferes with a ball in play shall be ejected from the ballpark," Pirates manager Danny Murtaugh was supposedly heard muttering, "I just hope that Stuart doesn't think that includes him."

All in all, when you look at the handicap that Mazeroski faced for several of his big-league seasons, it seems that induction into the Hall of Fame represents a final balancing of the scales of justice.

Yankee sluggers Mickey Mantle (right) and Roger Maris met their match in Bill Mazeroski during the 1960 fall classic. Maz, a Pittsburgh Pirates infielder, became the first player to end a World Series with a home run.

The first batter in the bottom of the ninth was Bill Mazeroski, who was highly regarded for his glove work. In blue-collar Pittsburgh this made him a man to be admired. Pittsburgh was a town with a work ethic, and glamour boys were looked on with suspicion. Maz was one of the greatest defensive second basemen in the history of baseball, a man who turned a position-record 1,706 double plays. They called him "no hands" and "no touch," so fluid and graceful was his transfer of the ball from glove to throwing hand on the relay to first. Maz's lifetime batting average of .260 was unlikely to strike terror in the hearts of anyone, least of all the wrecking crew from New York, but he was no pushover either, as evidenced by his game-winning homer in Game 1 and other key Series hits.

Ralph Terry, the Yankees' fifth pitcher of the afternoon, looked in at Mazeroski. The first pitch was a fastball, high and inside, and Maz let it go by. Yankees catcher Johnny Blanchard trotted to the mound and told Terry to get the next pitch down. Terry wound up and threw a slider, and the ball crossed the plate at the letters. The modest second baseman swung and propelled a long drive to left field that cleared the wall above outfielder Yogi Berra's head. The crowd rose as one, erupting into spontaneous celebration. It was Pittsburgh's first world championship in 35 years.

When the dust had settled and the cheering had moved from Forbes Field to the streets of Pittsburgh, the statisticians, as is their wont, attempted to analyze the result and quantify the drama—never a good idea when the human variables of desire and heart are there to skew the results.

arsenal. They won the blowouts; the Pirates won the squeakers. Appropriately, the underdog Pirates began with a two-run homer by Rocky Nelson. But the Yankees were far from throwing in the towel and answered with a home run by Bill Skowron in the fifth and another by Yogi Berra in the sixth. The Yankees led, 5–4, after six innings. In the bottom of the eighth inning, the Pirates recaptured the lead, 9–7, on a three-run homer by Hal Smith. However, the never-say-die New Yorkers came back to tie the game in the top of the ninth, and the two combatants staggered toward the bottom of the ninth and baseball immortality.

On paper, the Pirates were slaughtered in the 1960 World Series. On paper, the Yanks won by an average score of 8–4. Statistically, the Yankees were baseball's version of the man who drowned in a pool with an average depth of five feet. During the seven-game barrage, the Yankees scored 28 more runs than the Bucs and forged a new Series record for team batting with a torrid .338 mark. The Pirates batted a tepid .256. The Yankees sprayed out 91 hits; the Bucs managed 60, an amazing 31-hit differential.

But games are not played on paper.

When Maz's homer went over the ivy-covered left-field wall, it was tempting to report that the Yankees, who had lived by the sword, died the same way. Actually, during the seven-game battle, the Yankees had inflicted several usually fatal wounds, but they eventually died from a series of strategically inflicted paper cuts.

Oh yes, remember Spike and Chester? It was Chester who won the day and Spike who ended up prancing around him looking for respect. Miraculous Mazeroski, the Pirates' own M&M boy, had won the game—and the Series—the Yankee way, with a home run in the bottom of the ninth.

Mazeroski is rushed by exuberant teammates and fans at home plate.

Whitey Ford squared the series at 3–3 as the Yanks romped to a 12–0 win with 17 hits. Earlier Ford had pitched the Yankees to a 10–0 win in the third game, all of which made the seventh game possible. Had it not been for Ford's pitching, Maz would never have had the opportunity to make the history books with his Series-winning homer.

Munich Clock Controversy
September 9, 1972, Rudi-Sedlmayer Halle, Munich

This was an Olympics mired in politics and controversy. It was summer 1972 and the twentieth Olympic Games were under way in Munich, Germany. The Americans had high hopes for their basketball team. Why wouldn't they? The United States had gone unbeaten in 62 straight Olympic Games, winning seven gold medals over 36 years.

But this was an Olympics interrupted by tragedy. On September 5, with only six days left in the Games, 8 Palestinian terrorists snuck into the Olympic Village and seized 11 Israeli team members, demanding the release of 200 Palestinians that were being held in Israel. The terror continued for almost 24 hours before a rescue attempt ensued, but in the end, all 11 Israelis were killed along with 5 of the terrorists.

Amid a flurry of controversy, the International Olympic Committee decided the Games should continue. Olympic flags were lowered to half-mast, and 80,000 mourners attended a memorial service while competition was suspended for 24 hours. When the Olympiad resumed, nothing was quite the same.

"The Games continued," explained John E. Lacey, head trainer for the U.S. team, "but they didn't have their luster. The enthusiasm died down."

Everyone knew the U.S. basketball team was unbeatable. They cruised through their early matchups, easily beating Czechoslovakia, Australia, Cuba, Brazil, Egypt, Spain, Japan, and Italy. Only one team stood between them and the gold medal—the USSR.

The game was remarkable in several ways. This was before the days of America's "Dream Team." In 1972, the U.S. squad was composed of college players. Talented, yes, but definitely not professionals.

Due to an agreement with ABC-TV, the tip-off was scheduled for 11:45 P.M. in Munich, allowing millions of fans to watch the events unfold from their living rooms. "If you are too young, or unaware of the story of the 1972 U.S. Olympic basketball team, you would probably guess their story is too bizarre to be true," said Rick Bernstein, executive producer of HBO Sports, who produced an HBO presentation revisiting the dramatic event.

"It was sort of like celebrating on top of the Sears Tower in Chicago and then being thrown off and falling 100 floors to the ground. That's the kind of emptiness and sick feeling I felt."
—U.S. Olympic basketball team guard Doug

Featuring a pair of teams that were 8–0, the Americans and Soviets were happy to provide the drama. The USSR took a 7–0 lead and held on with a 26–21 advantage at halftime.

Emotions ran high and the play was physical. With 12:18 left on the clock, the Soviets were ahead, 38–34, when a loose-ball scuffle ensued. USSR reserve Dvorni Edeshko and the USA's Dwight Jones were ejected from the game. Jones, a 6'9" Houston center, was the U.S. team's top scorer and rebounder.

During the subsequent jump ball, 6'9" Minnesota forward Jim Brewer became another U.S. team casualty. He was knocked to the floor and suffered a concussion, forcing him to leave the game.

The USSR was still leading by eight points with 6:07 remaining, but the Americans were not about to give up. They

MAKING THE CALL

Most sports fans have gone to a game or event where they found themselves complaining about the officiating. Some fans, in fact, do almost nothing *but* complain about the calls that are made.

Most of the time when a questionable call is made, a coach complains and the next call is in favor of his or her team. It all evens out in the end. Every now and then, however, a controversial call changes the outcome of the game. One such game was the 1972 Olympic basketball finals between the United States and the Soviet Union. And fans are still bitter.

The controversy surrounding this game is so great that in 2002 HBO Sports produced a documentary featuring the events that took place 30 years earlier in Munich. "In this documentary we reexamine the events that fueled this superpower basketball showdown, as well as the stunning turn of events in the final three seconds of the game," said Rick Bernstein, the show's producer. The show also features several of the players involved in the game in 1972, along with sports announcers and journalists who covered the matchup live.

Sometimes time softens disappointments. Sometimes people can look back years down the road and see events more objectively. But neither of these were the case with the great Olympic basketball controversy. There was no gray area here. Everyone present had an opinion, and that opinion has not changed in 30 years.

All of the Russians interviewed were convinced that their team won. Each American felt the same. The Soviets were particularly upset and disappointed that the Americans refused to attend the medal ceremony or pick up their medals. For their part, the Americans all felt strongly that the silver medals did not belong to them. Some of the players went so far as to add a clause to their wills stating that their descendants could never accept the silver medals after their death.

We may never know who really won. Or who should have won. But as one American broadcaster said, the real question is why a game of this magnitude was run so poorly. It was the gold-medal game in an Olympics that begged a hero. It was televised worldwide. And it was officiated by a couple of referees who couldn't speak the same language. They couldn't communicate with the timekeepers, the players, the coaches, or even each other. Is there any wonder that confusion reigned?

1972 USA RESULTS (8–1)

USA	66	Czechoslovakia	35
USA	81	Australia	55
USA	67	Cuba	48
USA	61	Brazil	54
USA	96	Egypt	31
USA	72	Spain	56
USA	96	Japan	33
USA	68	Italy	38
USSR	51	USA	50

1972 OLYMPIC GAMES FINAL STANDINGS

USSR (9–0)	Brazil (5–4)	Philippines (3–6)
USA (8–1)	Czechoslovakia (4–5)	Japan (2–7)
Cuba (7–2)	Australia (5–4)	Senegal (0–8)
Italy (5–4)	Poland (3–6)	Egypt (0–8)
Yugoslavia (7–2)	Spain (4–5)	
Puerto Rico (6–3)	F.R. of Germany (3–6)	

the basket for a layup. Instead, he was fouled and went to the line to shoot two.

Collins took a breath and sunk one shot and then the other, giving the United States a one-point lead of 50–49 with just three seconds left on the clock. After that, confusion reigned.

The Soviets inbounded the ball to midcourt, when Brazilian referee Renato Righetto blew his whistle to stop the play with one second remaining. The crowd stormed the court in celebration of the American win, but they were quickly disbursed by Righetto, who had noticed a disturbance at the scorer's table and halted play to determine the problem.

Apparently the USSR coach, Vladimir Kondrashkin, claimed that he had called for a timeout after Collins' first free throw. The clock was reset to three seconds and the Soviets were given a second chance to inbound the ball.

This time the pass was short, the Soviets failed to score, and the Americans again began to celebrate. But it wasn't over yet.

The clock had not been reset properly and Great Britain's R. William Jones, secretary-general of the International Amateur Basketball Federation (FIBA), stepped in and ordered the clock to be reset to three seconds—again.

Ivan Edeshko took the ball out of bounds, where he was guarded by 6'11" forward Tom McMillen of Maryland. The referee motioned to McMillen to back up, and he moved back nearly to midcourt. The referee, who spoke only Armenian at the time, later said he only meant for the American player to move back a few inches, but his gesture said something else to McMillen, who didn't want to risk a foul or ejection at this crucial moment. Unfortunately, his move enabled Edeshko to make a long pass

Team USA's Dwight Jones tries to grab the ball as a Russian player goes for a score during the 1972 basketball final at the Olympic Games in Munich.

closed the gap to 49–48 on a Jim Forbes jumper with 40 seconds on the clock.

The Soviets hung onto the ball while the clock ticked down to just 10 seconds remaining before attempting another shot. Tom McMillen blocked Aleksander Belov's shot, and Doug Collins, a guard out of Illinois State, drove to

United States basketball team players enjoy a brief moment of elation, thinking they have beaten the Soviets, but soon after the referee reset the clock by three seconds and the Soviet Union scored a final goal to win the game, 51–50.

the length of the court to star player Aleksander Belov. Belov pushed past two defenders to make an easy layup and score the winning points as the buzzer sounded.

The United States filed a protest before the Jury of Appeals, but it was denied on a 3–2 vote, with judges from three communist countries siding with the Soviets. The USSR was awarded the gold medal for the first time in Olympic basketball history.

The U.S. team voted unanimously to refuse their silver medals. "We didn't win silver, we won gold," one player said. The tissue-wrapped medals still sit today in a wooden drawer in Olympic headquarters.

Russia's Aleksander Belov scores the winning basket to push his team past the United States.

Fisk Waves It Fair

October 21, 1975, Fenway Park, Boston

Many baseball observers claim Game 6 of the 1975 World Series was the greatest baseball game ever played. It certainly had all the elements: spectacular—even courageous—fielding plays, clutch hitting, sudden-death drama, and enough heroes to fill an entire wing at Cooperstown. But the lasting image is that of heroic Carlton Fisk, New England's gift to baseball folklore. It is a game in which Fisk did as much for body English as Shakespeare did for the written variety.

The 1975 World Series contenders were a study in contrasts: the decidedly underdog Red Sox pitted against possibly the best team ever assembled, the 1975 Cincinnati Reds. Neither team had captured a world championship since the Kaiser was causing problems in Germany. The 1975 Sox were an odd mix of veterans and youngsters just up from the farm. In fact, the Red Sox had ridden into the postseason on the backs of two rookie sensations, Jim Rice and Fred Lynn. Rice, however, had suffered a season-ending wrist injury. Future Hall of Famer Carl Yastrzemski was still hungry—*famished* may be a better word—for his first World Series title, but he was on the downside of his career. Dwight "Dewey" Evans was a force at the plate and undeniably so in right field. Shortstop Rick Burleson was solid, as was Denny Doyle at second, and veteran Rico Petrocelli remained a fixture at third. Catcher Fisk was a great handler of pitchers, a great defensive catcher, and a determined, if deliberate, force at the plate. The pitching rotation included Luis Tiant, whose age was somewhere between 35 and social security, and Bill "Spaceman" Lee, who marched to his own offbeat drummer.

The veteran Reds—the vaunted Big Red Machine—had dominated the National League in 1975, winning an incredible 108 games and capturing the NL West by a ridiculous 20 games. They swept aside the Pittsburgh Pirates in three straight games in the National League Conference Series. They boasted Pete Rose, Tony Perez, spark plug Joe Morgan, Johnny Bench, George Foster, and defensive standout Davey Concepcion. Their pitching staff was almost as impressive.

The Series was a seesaw affair, but traveling back to Beantown for Game 6, the Reds were leading three games to two,

> ## "I was going to make sure I stepped on every little white thing out there, even if I had to straight-arm or kick somebody to do it."
>
> ### —Red Sox catcher Carlton Fisk

and the Sox were on the brink of elimination. What the Sox needed was a good old-fashioned miracle, maybe a plague of locusts to descend on the Reds, or boils to render them helpless. Alas, no such miracle was on the horizon, only ominous storm clouds. Suddenly the rains came, bringing the World Series to a screeching halt. One sodden day passed. And another. And yet another.

On October 21, the sun broke through the clouds, and the only thunder forecast was from the Reds' potent bats. If there was a pot of gold at the end of the rainbow that followed the deluge, it was in the form of potbellied, 24-carat, cigar-chomping Luis Tiant. Now rested, Tiant, already the winner in Boston's two previous Series victories, was chosen to start the game for the Red Sox against Gary Nolan.

Boston jumped out to a quick 3–0 lead on a Freddie Lynn homer in the bottom half of the first inning. Meanwhile, Tiant was brilliant. Using his now-you-see-it, now-you-don't delivery and a

GAME 6 MAGIC

In the oasis-like greenery of Fenway Park, in the twelfth inning of Game 6, at precisely 34 minutes after midnight on October 22, 1975, only two objects in Fenway Park mattered to anyone in attendance. One was inanimate, the left-field foul pole standing to the left of the Green Monster; the other was Carlton Fisk, very animated indeed as he skipped down the first-base line thrusting his arms toward fair territory like someone deranged.

The result of all the body English and the combined will of Red Sox Nation produced results so magical that they would have impressed both Uri Geller and Harry Potter. The ball kept fading left, left, left . . . but ultimately hit the mesh screen attached to the foul pole. The umpire signaled a home run and a Red Sox victory.

Apparently everyone from southern New Hampshire to northern Nova Scotia was aboard for the ride. And who can blame them? It was one of those milestone moments in so many lives, like the day you learned to ride a bike or your first kiss.

Game 7 should be mentioned in the Funk and Wagnalls under *anticlimactic*. For the record, the Red Sox lost that game and the 1975 World Series. They jumped to an early lead, scoring three runs in the third inning. Cincinnati responded in the sixth with two of their own, courtesy of a Tony Perez homer, and another in the seventh to tie it. They won the game, 4–3, on a bloop single by Joe Morgan, giving the venerable franchise its first world title in 35 years. It was a great day in Reds' history. But Game 6 arguably did more for the Boston Red Sox than any single game in their history. It made believers out of a whole generation of young fans and made the Boston Red Sox—for a while, at least—America's Team.

Carlton Fisk slams a twelfth-inning home run to give Boston a victory in the sixth game of the 1975 World Series. The catcher is Cincinnati's Johnny Bench and the umpire is Dave Davidson.

Fisk reacts as he sees his home run hit the left-field foul pole.

his feet and received a warm ovation as he shook off the effects of the collision. When the game resumed, Bench hit another Tiant offering off the Green Monster to score Griffey and pull the Reds into a 3–3 tie. In the seventh and eighth, the Reds scored three more times, building a seemingly insurmountable three-run lead, leaving the score 6–3.

The impending defeat had temporarily silenced the usually raucous Fenway crowd. In the bottom of that same eighth inning, though, an unlikely star emerged. With two men on and two outs, utility man and future hairdresser Bernie Carbo came to the plate to pinch hit against Reds master reliever Rawly Eastwick. Carbo worked the count full, then awkwardly fought off another tough inside delivery. Then, to the astonishment and delight of the Fenway faithful, Carbo tied the game with a single swing of the bat, a powerful drive that cleared the high wall in deep center more than four hundred feet away.

The Red Sox teased their fans in the ninth inning by loading the bases with none out but failing to score. In the top of the eleventh, Joe Morgan, the mighty mite of the Reds lineup, launched a ball toward the deepest reaches of right field. Going full out toward the wall, Dewey Evans leaped and pulled the ball and the game back from the abyss, and then unleashed his golden arm to double the runner off first base and end the Reds' threat. Inspiring for the Sox, demoralizing for the Reds.

Then, just when it seemed every last dram of emotion had been wrung from the dishtowel crowd, Carlton Fisk walked to the plate in the twelfth inning to face Pat Darcy, the eighth Reds pitcher of the game. Fisk was the

windup that resembled a bizarre ballet, he allowed just one hit and no runs in the first four innings of work. But in the fifth the Reds seemed to have figured out his conjurer's tricks, scoring three runs grouped around a Ken Griffey drive that bounded away from Fred Lynn as Lynn collided with Fenway's then-unpadded center-field wall. Fenway became funereal as spectators craned their necks to watch their fallen hero. Finally, after what seemed an eternity, the rookie was helped to prototypical New England hero—a man of sturdy Yankee (no, not *those* Yankees) stock. He had the work ethic of a lumberjack and the spontaneity of a back-porch whittler. He settled into the batter's box with a stiff, deliberate style that lacked the fluidity of Yaz or Lynn or Rice. He was almost robotic in his movements. Boston fans loved these kinds of no-nonsense athletes, guys who didn't alibi when they lost or boast when they won, guys who were reticent with the press and worked their tails off on the field. Superstars have always taken heat in Beantown, from Ted to Yaz to Rice to Russell to Bledsoe. The blue-collar guys, especially if they hail from places like Bellows Falls, Vermont, are the only ones who are above criticism.

As Fisk's ball hit the foul pole and was therefore signaled a homer, all the pent-up emotions of 57 years of frustration were vented in Fenway and in homes across the northeastern United States. The Red Sox had won, 7–6. Longtime Fenway Park organist John Kiley played the "Hallelujah Chorus" and fans responded as if they were caught up in a kind of religious fervor. Boston had come out on top in a four-hour Wagnerian opera, and when the fat lady sang, she sang to Kiley's accompaniment.

Fisk jumps on home plate after hitting the homer that won the sixth game of the World Series.

10

Flutie's Hail Mary

November 23, 1984, the Orange Bowl, Miami

Doug Flutie knew exactly what he wanted to do. The trick was going out onto the field and actually doing it.

The Miami Hurricanes had taken a 45–41 lead over Flutie and the Boston College Eagles with 28 seconds to play in Miami's Orange Bowl. Boston College's possession was beginning at their own 20-yard line.

"I told my teammates I just wanted to get near midfield," Flutie said. "I feel if I get there I have a 50-50 chance of scoring. I said, 'We've got at least four plays. Let's get the ball out near midfield and put one up in the end zone.'"

It took three plays for the Eagles to move to the Miami 48. There were now six seconds remaining on the clock, time for one more play. Flutie called for the "Flood Tip" play, in which three receivers converge in the end zone, with the intention that one will try to tip the ball to another. The play had worked once earlier in the year, against Temple.

Flutie took the snap, but he had to move toward his right out of the pocket because of the Miami rush. He saw the receivers heading for the end zone, and from his own 37-yard line he let the ball fly as the clock ticked down to zero.

One receiver was his roommate, Gerard Phelan, who already had caught 10 passes in the game.

"We both think about these kinds of finishes," Flutie said, "but we don't talk about them to each other."

As Phelan saw the ball coming toward him, he also realized he was behind the Miami defensive backs. Instead of tipping the ball, he caught it and held on as he fell into the end zone, answering the Hail Mary prayer that gave Boston College a 47–45 victory. The extra point was not attempted.

"He just threw a rocket," Phelan said. "I held that thing against my shoulder pads like it was my firstborn."

Said Boston College coach Jack Bicknell, "The pass was supposed to come down to Phelan, and he's supposed to tip it to someone else. But if it hits you in the chest, you catch it."

For a few seconds, Flutie did not have any idea what had happened once he released the ball.

"I didn't see anything much until the referee raised his arms," Flutie said. "Then, I admit, I couldn't believe it, except when everybody started yelling and pulling me up."

"I thought I was dead, but I was thinking to myself, 'What a way to go!'"
—Boston receiver Gerard Phelan

Flutie's pass traveled a remarkable 64 yards in the air and capped a remarkable day that saw him complete 34 of 46 passes for 472 yards and three touchdowns as he outdueled Miami sophomore Bernie Kosar. Playing before a national television audience the day after Thanksgiving, Flutie's performance likely earned him the extra votes he needed to win the 1984 Heisman Trophy.

"I guess the defenders didn't think Doug could throw the ball that far, and I knew he could," Phelan said. "As he threw it, the ball was coming down, and as everybody jumped up in front of me, the ball disappeared for a moment and there was a lot of contact. All of a sudden the ball reappeared, probably in the last three yards. It was one of those things where you react as quick as you can. Just like a fork falls off a table, you react to catch it. I happened to get it."

Phelan said he didn't know if the play would work, but he knew Flutie would give it everything he had.

STANDING TALL

After a stellar career as a Boston College Eagle—and winning the Heisman Trophy as a junior—Doug Flutie was slated to be taken in the first three rounds of the 1985 National Football League draft. But the speedy field general opted instead to sign with the USFL's New Jersey Generals for what was at the time a record contract for a rookie in any professional sports league. Flutie only collected on one year of the six-year, 8.3 million dollar deal before the league folded.

Flutie joined the Chicago Bears, who were coming off a dominant season and a Super Bowl victory, for the 1987 season. He was stuck on the bench throughout that season, as well as the next two, which he spent in New England with the Patriots.

Unable to break through into the NFL quarterback ranks, Flutie sought to resuscitate his career by traveling north of the border to the Canadian Football League. He joined the British Columbia Lions in 1990, and had a respectable season at the helm of that team.

The next season, respectable began to change into legendary as Flutie launched an all-out assault on the CFL record books. Throughout eight seasons in the CFL, Flutie won the league's championship—the Grey Cup—three times and was named the league's Most Outstanding Player a record six times.

Flutie broke back into the NFL for the 1998 season and took it by storm, stirring Buffalo into a frenzy as a spark plug behind the center. He stayed in Buffalo for three years, becoming a national icon with his Flutie Flakes and his work for charity.

Flutie joined the San Diego Chargers for the 2001 season, helping to turn around the floundering franchise. Now mentoring the Chargers' young quarterback, Drew Brees, Flutie continues to work for his charity, the Doug Flutie Jr. Foundation for Autism.

"Most players I've seen, when they get into that kind of position, give up," Phelan said. "I don't think anybody on our team really thought that way from the beginning of the play to the end."

It seemed for a while that the team that had the ball last was going to win, and that's how the game turned out. There were four lead changes in the fourth quarter alone.

Kosar was almost as brilliant as Flutie, completing 25 of 38 passes for 447 yards and two touchdowns. Eddie Brown of Miami had 10 receptions for 220 yards, and running back Melvin Bratton gained 134 yards on the ground and scored four touchdowns, including the score with 28 seconds left that Miami thought was going to give the Hurricanes the victory.

Instead, Boston College's improbable victory over the defending national champion Hurricanes improved the Eagles' record for the year to 8–2, its most successful year since 1942, and secured a trip to the Cotton Bowl. During the game, Flutie also became the first college quarterback in history to surpass the 10,000 passing yards mark for his career.

Doug Flutie was the object of everyone's affection after his roommate, Gerard Phelan, caught a last-second desperation pass—the "Hail Flutie." Phelan had already caught 10 passes in the game before this big one.

Second Team

11

Havlicek's Steal

April 15, 1965, Boston Garden, Boston

John Havlicek, who scored more than 30,000 points in 16 magnificent seasons with the Boston Celtics from 1962–63 through 1977–78, ironically is best remembered for none of those points, but rather for a steal he made against the arch rival Philadelphia 76ers in Game 7 of the 1965 NBA Eastern Division Finals.

The NBA in 1965 was a far different league from what it is today. There were only nine teams then, and they seemed to play each other every week. Such familiarity breeds heated rivalries, if not contempt, and no rivalry was more heated than the one between the Celtics and the 76ers. Boston was the top dog, having won six consecutive championships under the guidance of the wily Red Auerbach, with a team built around brilliant center Bill Russell. Philadelphia, tired of playing second fiddle, had swung a trade on January 15, 1965, to acquire massive center Wilt Chamberlain for the express purpose of battling Russell. Though they won only 40 regular-season games to Boston's 62, Philadelphia was coming together as the playoffs began and seemed poised to dethrone the Celtics.

The home team won each of the first six games of the best-of-seven series, holding serve, if you will.

It looked as though the pattern would continue in Game 7, as the Celtics took a five-point lead into the final minutes of the game at storied Boston Garden. But Philadelphia rallied, cutting it to one at 110–109 with five seconds to play.

All Boston needed to do was pass the ball inbounds and run out the clock, but Russell's toss from under the basket hit one of the guide wires that ran down from the ceiling to help support the backboard. Referee Earl Strom called the violation and awarded possession to Philadelphia, who took a timeout. For the final play, Philadelphia coach Dolph Schayes thought about the obvious, getting the ball to Chamberlain, but chose another option. "Wilt's problems at the foul line weighed on my mind, so I set up a play where Hal Greer would pass the ball to Chet Walker, and Johnny Kerr would set a pick to free Walker for a shot," said Schayes.

> ## "Greer is putting the ball into play. He gets it out deep. Havlicek steals it. Over to Sam Jones. Havlicek stole the ball! It's all over! Johnny Havlicek stole the ball!"
> —broadcaster Johnny Most

Greer, with five seconds to put the ball in play, looked toward the 7'1" Chamberlain in the low post but the smaller, quicker Russell moved in front of Chamberlain, making a pass into the pivot too risky. Meanwhile, Boston's K. C. Jones was leaping along the baseline and frantically waving his arms to distract Greer. The Philadelphia guard jumped and spotted Walker out beyond the key, seemingly in the open. But Havlicek, always a savvy defender, had taken a position several feet off the direct line of sight between Greer and Walker, making it look like Walker was free when really he wasn't.

Havlicek remembered it all clearly in the book *When Seconds Count* (by Alex Sachare, published in 1999 by Sports Publishing Inc.). "When he was having trouble putting it in play," said Havlicek, "I had a vision as to where the ball was and where my man was. I was counting, and when I got to 'one thousand and four,' I took a peek over my shoulder and saw that Greer

THE SIXTH MAN

It doesn't matter who starts the game; it's who finishes that counts.

That was one of the coaching precepts of Red Auerbach, the architect of the Boston Celtics dynasty and the man for whom the NBA's Coach of the Year trophy is named. Auerbach guided the Celtics to 8 championships in a row, 11 in 13 seasons, and when he retired to the Celtics front office in 1966, he was the NBA's winningest coach, with 938 victories in the regular season and 99 more in the playoffs.

Auerbach knew the importance of a strong bench, of reserves who could come in and not only protect a lead but also extend it or overcome a deficit. And key to this effort was his "sixth man," a player often talented enough to be in the starting lineup but who was kept on the bench so he could step in and swing the momentum of a game. Invariably, that player would also be on the court in the closing minutes of a tight game, while one of the starters watched from the bench.

"Psychologically, as soon as you pull one of your five starters out of the game, the other team is going to let down just a bit," explained Auerbach. "That's when I wanted a guy like Ramsey or Havlicek to get out there and run them into the ground."

Frank Ramsey, a 6'3" guard who averaged 13.4 points per game in 10 seasons, was the first of Auerbach's great sixth men. But the man best known for his play in that role is John Havlicek. A defensive standout on an Ohio State team that was led by high-scoring Jerry Lucas, the 6'5" Havlicek was such a versatile and talented athlete that he was drafted in 1962 as a wide receiver by the NFL's Cleveland Browns even though he never played football in college.

Havlicek was ideal for the role of sixth man, since he was capable of playing guard or forward and affecting a game at either end of the court. He would average 20.8 points and 6.3 rebounds per game over 20 NBA seasons and make the league's All-Defensive first or second team eight times. Eventually, his skills would force Auerbach to make him a starter, but it was Havlicek's proficiency as a sixth man in his first four NBA seasons that enabled him to develop into a Hall of Fame player.

Boston's Bill Russell shoots over Philadelphia's Wilt Chamberlain in the first quarter.

had. She asked me if I recognized the material. I didn't. She told me it was a piece of my uniform that someone had gotten that night."

The Celtics would go on to beat the Los Angeles Lakers in five games for the championship, their seventh in an NBA-record string of eight in a row and eleven in thirteen seasons. But the Lakers series was anticlimactic after the brilliant ending to the Boston-Philly showdown in the Division Finals.

It was while listening to the radio on the day after the win over Philadelphia that Havlicek began to realize that his steal might become his basketball legacy.

"The incident would have been remembered as just one of the many big things the Celtics have been involved with," said Havlicek, "except that our announcer, Johnny Most, went almost completely haywire at the end of the game." Indeed, the call by the gravel-voiced Most ranks in the pantheon of sports broadcasting, right up there with Al Michaels' "Do you believe in miracles?" from the USA hockey team's victory over the Soviets at the 1980 Olympics and Russ Hodges' "The Giants win the pennant! The Giants win the pennant!" from baseball's 1951 National League playoffs.

Most started his call off slowly, warily, as if sensing impending doom with Philadelphia having a chance to end Boston's reign. "Greer is putting the ball into play. He gets it out deep," Most intoned cautiously, fearing the worst for his beloved Celtics.

Then, suddenly, Most started screaming in a frenzy that matched what was taking place on the court: "Havlicek steals it!" he cried. "Over to Sam Jones. Havlicek stole the ball! It's all

was about to lob a pass to Walker. I knew that I would have a good chance of deflecting or intercepting it. I made a controlled deflection to Sam Jones, who was right near me. He went down the sideline, dribbling out the clock, and the game was over. As soon as the buzzer went off, the crowd went bananas.

"It was hysteria and euphoria. Fans were grabbing me and a couple of fans ripped off my jersey. Years later, I went to a party and a woman came up to me and showed me this brooch she over! Johnny Havlicek stole the ball!" Throughout the pandemonium, Most kept repeating that phrase, "Havlicek stole the ball," over and over.

"I didn't realize it was that outstanding a play until I heard Johnny Most," Havlicek would later say. "The next day, radio station WHDH, which did our games in those days, kept repeating the tape of the game ending, including Johnny Most's semihysterical call. All over Greater Boston, the phrase, 'Havlicek stole the ball,' came to mean a great deal. That play has gotten bigger and bigger as time goes on."

Throughout the Series, Boston's John Havlicek (left) was all over Philadelphia's Chet Walker (center).

12

Buckner's Boot

October 25, 1986, Shea Stadium, Flushing, New York

E-3. It doesn't look like much in a box score, but tell that to Red Sox Nation. It's engraved deeply in their psyches, a scar on their souls. All across New England, there are scattered hundreds of people who believe they are the ones who jinxed the Red Sox in 1986. "I called my brother-in-law on the phone to make sure he was watching." "I woke up my four-year-old to make sure he saw it, the first time the Red Sox had won since 1918." "I set off a string of fireworks just before Wilson grounded out to first." The problem, of course, was that Mookie Wilson did not ground out to first. The wrong Boston player was covering the first-base bag, and the ball failed to take the expected third hop and skittered under his glove, right through his legs, allowing Ray Knight to score the winning run all the way from second. All season long, when it came to the late innings, Dave Stapleton had been put in at first for defensive purposes. This one night, however, Boston manager John McNamara apparently went with his heart and thought it would be nice to leave Bill Buckner on the field so that Billy Bucks could celebrate the World Series victory he'd done so much to help the Sox enjoy.

"Don't do me any more favors like that," Buckner might well have told McNamara later. Instead of credit being given him for his 102 runs batted in during the 1986 regular season, and in spite of the leadership he offered the team, playing through pain all year long, the name Bill Buckner will forever be linked with the one play he didn't make, and Buckner himself has to live out his life knowing his image is bound up with that one moment. And those Red Sox fans all across New England have to see the play unfold, year after year on television, and carry with themselves the knowledge that they personally jinxed the Sox. These are hard burdens to bear.

It was quite a Series. The Mets lost the first two games at home—a 1–0 gem won by Boston's Bruce Hurst in Game 1 and a 9–3 crusher after that. Sox fans, still high after the American League Championship Series win over the Angels, were exultant: a 2–0 lead coming home to Fenway Park! As fate would have it—funny how many championship teams really *are* good teams—the Mets came back and took the next two in Boston. Neither game was close: 7–1 and 6–2. Boston bounced back,

> # "The players don't have a goat, or one thing that everyone talks about. We just look at a lot of times in a ballgame where we should have done better. A lot of things happened before Bill Buckner missed the ground ball."
>
> ## —Red Sox outfielder Dave Henderson

though, with a 4–2 win, a complete-game effort by Bruce Hurst. As they shuttled back to Shea Stadium, the Sox had to win just one game to become world champions for the first time in 68 years.

Boston scored right off the bat, in the first inning. Boston scored in the second as well. Each time it was just one run, but after four and a half innings, it was 2–0 Red Sox. Roger Clemens was on the mound. He'd been 24–4 in the regular season, with a league-leading ERA of 2.48. But he gave up two runs in the fifth, and the game was tied. The Red Sox regained the lead with a run in the seventh, on a throwing error by Ray Knight—a candidate for the goat horns. But New York knotted it up again in the

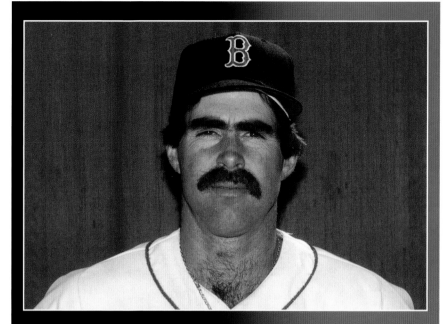

Before he was on the Red Sox, Bill Buckner lived in a converted church in Chicago, where he played for the Cubs. Perhaps he should have prayed for support, not from above, but from his teammates.

Any rational person can understand that Roger Clemens, Rich Gedman, Calvin Schiraldi, and Bob Stanley all had something to do with the loss in Game 6. Let's not forget manager John McNamara, who sentimentally sent Buckner out there to play the bag at first when he should have routinely replaced him with late-inning defensive sub Dave Stapleton. Let's also not forget, in the big picture the Sox had to lose four games, not just one, to drop the Series. And most important, let's remember to give credit to the Mets, who played good, hard baseball and won not only Game 6 but Game 7 as well.

But no one watching that sixth game live, who saw that baseball skitter past Buckner's gimpy legs, can ever be truly rational about the moment. Sox fans were traumatized; Mets fans were giddy with ecstasy. Buckner bore the blame. He still bears it, like a scarlet letter. The fact that he was an exceptional, courageous major league player gets lost in the emotional shuffle. The ball was his! The Sox had won the Series! And, with an inch to spare, everything changed. Right?

Wrong! The Sox had not really won the Series. The score was tied at that point. Had Buckner bagged the ball and beaten Mookie to first, anything could have happened. Some other Sox player might have been harnessed with Boston's ultimate defeat. Boston— maybe Buckner himself—might have bounced back and won in a later inning.

He had gone 0-for-5 in Game 6, though: it wasn't a good night for him. But the team blew a two-run lead in the bottom of the tenth. Two outs and no one on and Buckner hadn't a thing to do with either of the first two runs, the two that set up the final play.

The man did rack up 2,715 major league hits. He played 22 seasons of major league ball and played through severe ankle pain from 1975 through 1990. He endured daily pain, icing his ankles before and after every game, even giving himself cortisone shots as needed. Thus he endured agony, and he endured infamy. He's become something of a folk hero to some in Beantown. He's even got a rock band in Boston named after him.

Boston Red Sox first baseman Bill Buckner is a picture of dejection as he leaves the field after committing an error that allowed the winning run to score during Game 6 of the 1986 World Series. The ball was hit by the New York Mets' Mookie Wilson.

bottom of the eighth when Boston bungled not just one but two bunts, and the game went into extra innings, tied 3–3. The hero of the ALCS, Dave Henderson, led off the Bosox in the tenth with another home run and, giving themselves a little insurance, the Sox pushed across another run as Marty Barrett singled in Wade Boggs, who had doubled. The Red Sox had left 14 men on base during the game, but the two-run lead seemed sufficient.

Red Sox reliever Calvin Schiraldi (let's not forget that in 51 innings in the regular season, he'd maintained a 1.41 earned run average) got the first two Mets batters, Wally Backman and Keith Hernandez, to fly out in the bottom of the inning. Now seemed the time to start to savor the sweet taste of

triumph. All it took was one more out and long-pent-up celebrations would break out all over New England. Mets first baseman Keith Hernandez had already given up and gone back into the clubhouse to console himself with a beer. The Shea scoreboard crew had conceded as well—they prematurely flashed the message they'd keyed up: "CONGRATULATIONS, RED SOX."

But it wasn't over yet. It's never over 'til it's over, according to Yogi. Gary Carter singled and so did Kevin Mitchell. Ray Knight later said, "When I came into the dugout in the bottom of the tenth, I grabbed a bat from the rack and hoped I'd get a chance to hit. I hoped that I'd get a chance to redeem myself for the error. I didn't want to be the goat who lost the last game of the World Series." Knight had been taken off the hook, of course, by the Mets in the eighth, but here he was, maybe the last batter of the year for the New York Mets. And Schiraldi had him down, 0–2. One strike was all that remained. Knight popped a single into center and put the Mets back in the game.

Bob Stanley was brought in to relieve the shaky Schiraldi, who'd surrendered three straight singles. Stanley's wild pitch on a 2–2 count to Mookie Wilson allowed Mitchell to scoot in from third. For the third time in this one game, the Mets had come from behind to tie the score. This time, they didn't stop there. The wild pitch brought the count to 3–2. Some blamed Rich Gedman for a passed ball, and Gedman's and Stanley's wives reportedly squared off afterward on the call, but the attribution didn't matter at the time. What mattered was shutting down the Mets before they scored again.

Isn't it what every kid dreams of—a 3–2 count in the bottom of the inning when a majestic home run could catapult your team to victory, winning the World Series? Well, Mookie Wilson did what a staggering percentage of hitters do on the 3–2 count: he fouled off the next pitch. Then he did it again.

When he did hit the ball fair, it was no arcing fly over the right-field fence. It was no Roy Hobbs drive into the lights. It was a poor, routine little bouncer that, well, let's let Bill Buckner tell it: "I knew it was going to be a close play at first, because the guy runs so well. The ball went skip, skip, skip and didn't come up. The ball missed my glove. I can't remember the last time I missed a ball like that, but I'll remember that one." Indeed he will. Forever.

The Series was tied at three each. There was another game to play, but like Game 7 of the 1975 Series, it was almost anticlimactic. Rain delayed it for a day. When game day arrived, things looked good for Boston once more. In the top of the second they took a 3–0 lead, which they held until the bottom of the sixth, when New York tied it with three of their own. The Mets added three more in the bottom of the seventh. The Sox scratched back with two in the top of the eighth, but it was too little and almost too late, and New York piled on a couple more in the bottom of the inning. The Mets never had to play the bottom of the ninth. They ran out onto the field in celebration as they shut down the Sox and earned themselves championship rings to treasure for all time.

Lee Mazzilli and Wilson (No. 1) celebrate after scoring the first two runs of Game 7 for the Mets on a single by Keith Hernandez during sixth-inning action.

13

Gibson in a Pinch

October 15, 1988, Dodger Stadium, Los Angeles

As a general rule, the climax—that very peak of excitement and drama—of the World Series is reserved for Game 6 or Game 7. Not so in 1988. Oddly enough, the climax for this Series occurred in Game 1, with the Dodgers' Kirk Gibson at the center of it. Gibson, signed in the off-season as a free agent from the Detroit Tigers, captured the 1988 National League MVP award despite batting under .300 and driving in a modest 76 runs. The controversial selection had outraged critics pointing to the superior numbers recorded by the Mets' Darryl Strawberry and others. The truth of the matter is that Gibson's selection had little to do with numbers at all. He won the award on intangibles, things like aggressive play and a winning attitude. As it turned out, the regular season was just the dress rehearsal for the postseason.

Gibson was so hobbled by injuries on opening night of the 1988 World Series, his legs were all but useless appendages. So unlikely a hero was the former Michigan State football star, he wasn't even supposed to be in the cast that day (although he could have used one to hold his leg together). Until the ninth inning, he had spent the entire game in the trainer's room.

In the bottom of the first inning, Mickey Hatcher hit a two-run home run to stake the Dodgers to a 2–0 lead over the heavily favored Oakland Athletics. A's strongman Jose Canseco responded with a grand slam in the top of the second, and the mighty A's were suddenly on top, 4–2. The Dodgers scratched back against intimidating Oakland starter Dave Stewart, scoring one run in the sixth inning, but they were unable to gain any further ground on the American League champs. Going into the bottom of the ninth down 4–3, things looked desperate for the Dodgers.

Dennis Eckersley, the toughest relief pitcher in baseball, with a 2.35 ERA and a league-best 45 saves, was on the mound for the A's. He quickly mowed down the first two Dodgers to face him before pinch-hitter Mike Davis drew a walk. The Dodgers' chances were hanging by a thread with Dodgers pitcher Alejandro Pena due up. Who would emerge from the dugout to take on the pinch-hitting challenge? Manager Tommy Lasorda's choices were few. He looked down the bench and pointed to Kirk Gibson. When Gibson hobbled up the stairs of

> ## "When he hit that ball it was surreal. As devastating a blow as it was, I remember running off the field and saying, 'Man, that was unbelievable.'"
> —A's shortstop Walt Weiss

the dugout and onto the field the effect was as shocking as Dracula emerging from his coffin. A buzz moved through the capacity crowd of 55,983 partisan fans.

The drama built as Gibson ran the count to 3–2. The next offering from Eckersley was a slider, and Gibson promptly hit it over the right-field wall to win the game and set off a wild night of celebration in Southern California.

Gibson showed such character that night, his teammates were motivated to turn in winning performances of their own. In Game 2 it was Orel Hershiser who starred, pitching a complete-game, three-hit masterpiece to defeat the A's, 6–0. In Game 3, away from Tinsel Town, Mark McGwire's solo homer in the bottom of the ninth provided the margin in a 2–1 victory for the A's. The Dodgers returned to form in Game 4, winning 4–3. Game 5 was another Hershiser gem, another complete-game

Kirk Gibson had other moments of high drama in a multifaceted career that saw him win World Series titles in both leagues. Tigers owner Tom Monaghan once said that Gibson was "a disgrace to the uniform with his beard and scruffy look," but his was the blue-collar face of a winner. Gibson never played in an All-Star Game, although he was twice selected for this honor (1985 and 1988). He was the ultimate team man, and individual statistics meant little to him.

His awesome power and rugged good looks prompted early comparisons with Mickey Mantle, and the expectations for Gibson were unreasonably high. Two things plagued him from the very beginning: a fiery temper and—like Mantle—a chronic propensity to leg injury. His temper was evident early on when he was sent to the Tigers' minor league team in Evansville rather than promoted to the majors, where he felt he belonged. He was often downright nasty with the press and regularly refused to sign autographs for fans. The fans respected Gibson's guts and hard work, but he was a tough guy to love.

Gibson treated the baseball diamond like a gridiron, throwing his body into harm's way without a second thought. Al Kaline worked hard to teach him the nuances of baseball defense and patience at the plate. Through motivational classes, Gibson learned to focus his aggressiveness in more positive ways, and the results were amazing. He led the Tigers to the pennant in 1984, hitting 27 homers and stealing 29 bases. That same year he was MVP of the ALCS, batting .417 against the Kansas City Royals. Gibson followed up by leading the Tigers past the San Diego Padres in the World Series, single-handedly destroying the Padres in the final game with five RBIs and two home runs. Padres fireballer Goose Gossage, who mistakenly believed he had Gibson's number, fought for the right to pitch to him, and then watched as his delivery disappeared into the ether, to seal the Detroit victory.

Gibson belted another 29 homers and stole 30 bases in 1985 and in 1986, despite recurring injuries, swiped 34 more while driving in 86 runs and swatting 28 homers. His numbers sagged in 1987 due to injuries, although he helped the Tigers to the AL Eastern Division title. He signed with the Dodgers the following year, just in time to bring his dramatic repertoire to Hollywood. He may have been an old hoofer, but he had experience on the postseason stage.

After his 1988 heroics, injuries continued to take their toll on Gibson. In 1993, he rejoined the Tigers and eventually retired midway through the 1995 season. His body could no longer take the punishment. The final record showed a .268 career batting average, 284 steals, and 255 home runs. What it doesn't show is a competitive heart as big as all outdoors. The heart of a winner.

effort that yielded just four hits and two runs as the Dodgers captured the World Series, four games to one.

Hershiser was the Series MVP, and few could argue with the selection of the winner of two World Series games. A strong case could also be made for Mickey Hatcher, who batted .368 with two HRs and five clutch RBIs, but there was little doubt in anyone's mind that it was the courageous home run of Kirk Gibson that had sparked the Dodgers to victory. When generations hence look back to the 1988 World Series, they need look no further than Game 1 to find the key to the Dodgers victory. Kirk Gibson made only one plate appearance in the entire World Series, but it was a genuine showstopper.

Los Angeles Dodgers pitcher Orel Hershiser (top) is lifted in the air by teammates. The Dodgers won four games to one in the Series against the A's.

Los Angeles Dodgers manager Tommy Lasorda (right) and Fred Claire, Dodgers vice president, hoist the World Series trophy following their team's decisive win.

Hershiser is shown in action against the Oakland Athletics during the decisive fifth game of the Series, at the Oakland Coliseum. Hershiser had two wins in the Series and was named World Series Most Valuable Player. The Dodgers beat the A's 5–2.

14

Laettner's Buzzer Beater

March 28, 1992, the Spectrum, Philadelphia

It took a perfect game to beat Kentucky in the 1992 East Regional Final, and that's what Duke got from Christian Laettner, college basketball's Player of the Year.

Duke, the defending national champion, had missed a chance to end the game and advance to its fifth straight Final Four when Bobby Hurley's 15-footer at the close of regulation rimmed out, forcing a five-minute overtime.

In overtime, the Blue Devils seemed headed for defeat when Kentucky guard Sean Woods drove past Hurley and banked home a 12-footer for a 103–102 lead. Duke called a timeout with 2.1 seconds left, and even though the Blue Devils had to go the length of the floor to score in that short amount of time, coach Mike Krzyzewski was calm and collected. "We all came to the huddle still burned by the shot that put Kentucky up," said Duke forward Grant Hill, "and Coach K had a plan already mapped out on the board. He said, 'OK, here's how we win the game: Grant, you throw to Christian here and he'll take the shot to win.' And that's exactly how it happened."

It's a play that every team has in its playbook, and one that almost never works, because not every team has players like Hill and Laettner to execute it.

As Hill prepared to take the ball out of bounds under his own basket, Laettner set up at the foul line at the opposite end of the Spectrum in Philadelphia, his back to the basket. Once Hill was handed the ball, the lanky, 6'11" Laettner—three inches taller than any

Kentucky player on the floor—spread his arms out wide to give his teammate as large a target as possible.

Hill winged a baseball pass some 75 feet, his aim true to the target. Kentucky's John Pelphrey made a move to try to intercept the pass, then backed off, fearing a foul call that would send Laettner to the line, where he already was a perfect 10-for-10. Then again, maybe he should have taken his chances, for Laettner hadn't missed any of his nine field-goal tries, either.

Laettner caught the pass with his back to the hoop, faked to his right, then took one dribble as he spun to his left. Pelphrey was off balance and Deron Feldhaus of Kentucky was anchored to the floor, too slow to react, as Laettner rose up and shot a 16-

"We just lost the greatest basketball game ever played."
—Kentucky guard Sean Woods

foot, right-handed jumper that seemed to hang in the air for several seconds before going through the net to give Duke the 104–103 victory.

"Totally incredible—I didn't even see it go in," said Laettner, who was engulfed by a swarm of Duke players and fans. On the Duke sideline, Krzyzewski had a different angle but the same view, or nonview. "As soon as he let it go, I knew it was going in," he said, "but I didn't see it because everyone jumped in front of me."

"I wanted them to make a lucky jump shot, a prayer," said Kentucky coach Rick Pitino—only this time Duke's prayer was answered.

Laettner's turnaround jumper completed one of the most remarkable performances in NCAA playoff history. He scored 31 points on 10-for-10 from the field, including his only three-point attempt, and 10-for-10 from the foul line. He also grabbed seven rebounds, playing 43 of a possible 45 minutes.

Duke led 50–45 after a fast-paced first half and seemed to be cruising with a 12-point advantage shortly before Laettner—the

FOR LAETTNER, IT WAS DÉJÀ VU
When Duke coach Mike Krzyzewski needed someone to take the last-second shot in overtime against Kentucky in the 1992 East Regional Final, he naturally turned to Christian Laettner. After all, the 6'11" senior had come through in an identical situation two years earlier.

In the 1990 East Regional Final at the Meadowlands, Duke was trailing Connecticut by one point in the closing seconds of overtime when Laettner got the ball on the right side and scored to give the Blue Devils a 79–78 victory and a trip to the Final Four. Laettner would go on to become the first collegian ever to start in four Final Fours and set an NCAA Tournament career scoring record with 407 points.

Laettner's ability to repeatedly come through in the clutch was no surprise to his coach. Laettner, who had won two state championships at the Nicholls School in Buffalo, New York, would win two NCAA titles at Duke and an Olympic gold medal as a member of the original Dream Team in 1992.

"Christian has this hunger for competition that I've never seen in anybody else," said Krzyzewski. "He's never afraid to make the play, be it a shot, rebound, pass, block, whatever. He wants to be there when the game is decided. "You've heard of guys who burn to win? This guy's got a forest fire inside him."

Duke University star Christian Laettner celebrates with teammate Grant Hill on the floor of the Philadelphia Spectrum as teammates and fans crowd around. Duke, the defending national champion, defeated the University of Kentucky to advance to the Final Four.

winner of the Wooden, Kodak, and Naismith Awards as well as college basketball's Player of the Year—was fouled by Aminu Timberlake of Kentucky. Timberlake fell to the floor, and as Laettner crossed over him, he stepped on the Kentucky player's stomach, drawing a technical foul and inciting the Wildcats.

Kentucky came roaring back, scoring nine straight points in one stretch to tie the score at 81 with 5:27 to play. It was close the rest of the way. With 1:02 left, Duke took a 93–91 lead on a jumper by Thomas Hill. Kentucky tied the

score when Feldhaus converted a Pelphrey miss with 38.6 seconds left. Hurley missed a driving jumper with two seconds left, and the game went into overtime, where the teams slugged it out like two heavyweights in the 15th round of a title fight.

Pelphrey hit a three-pointer at 3:58; Hurley answered with a trey at 2:40. Pelphrey sank two free throws at 2:17; Laettner matched them at 1:53, then put Duke up, 100–98, with a running eight-footer with 31.5 seconds left. Jamal Mashburn, Kentucky's All-American,

responded by converting a three-point play on a driving layup, giving the Wildcats a one-point lead with 19.6 seconds left. But Mashburn fouled out on the next play, and Laettner went to the line and converted two more free throws for a 102–101 lead. Just 14.1 seconds remained on the clock. Kentucky called a timeout with 7.2 seconds left to set up Woods' basket, which paved the way for the dramatic finish.

"It was a rare game, truly one of the best I've ever seen," said Georgia Tech coach Bobby Cremins. Echoed Wake Forest coach Dave Odom, "I don't know if I can find the right words to do the game justice. On the play at the end, it was a great pass and a great catch. But once those two are completed, you've got to have—*will* is not a strong enough word—one of the strongest constitutions in all of sport to take and make that shot."

"I can't believe it. Did that just happen?" Krzyzewski said in the interview room moments afterward. "There aren't enough adjectives to describe it. You can't write enough to tell about all the great plays that were made in that game. I told the kids in the locker room, I think we've just been a part of history. It's got to be somewhere in [David] Letterman's Top 10."

Laettner (No. 32) puts up his last-second, game-winning overtime jump shot over Kentucky's Deron Feldhaus to give Duke a 104–103 win in the 1992 NCAA east regional final in Philadelphia.

15

Triple-Overtime Thriller

June 4, 1976, Boston Garden, Boston

G ame 5 of the 1976 NBA Finals has become known as the "greatest game ever played." At the beginning of the season, however, no one would have anticipated this Finals matchup, much less the exciting events of Game 5.

Coming into the 1975–76 season, the Boston Celtics were very confident of their abilities and their place in the league. They had 12 world championships and a rich tradition behind them. They had loyal fans that filled the Boston Garden to watch their beloved team play on a beautiful parquet floor. And they had a goal—to play in the NBA Finals.

The Suns, on the other hand, were only an eight-year-old franchise. They had appeared in postseason play only one other time and lost in the first round. Five years had passed, and this year's team was primed for a return. But the experts had their own opinions. Many felt that Phoenix was the worst team in the league.

It was a season of ups and downs for the Suns. They started out in high style, winning 14 of 23 games, the best in franchise history. Unfortunately, the team was plagued with a series of injuries that sent them into a slump. They won only 4 of the next 22 games. Then came the All-Star break. It was the turning point for a team that was playoff-bound. They went 24–13 in the rest of the regular season, earning the right to play Seattle in the first round of the NBA playoffs.

Maybe it was the change in the lineup that gave the 1975–76 Suns their edge. An off-season trade got them Paul Westphal, and the draft secured two rookie starters in Alvan Adams and Ricky Sobers. Gar Heard was then acquired in a midseason deal on February 1. At the time, Phoenix was in last place, but that was about to change.

The opening round of the Finals began with the Suns beating the Seattle Supersonics four games to two. Their next hurdle would be the defending NBA champions—the Golden State Warriors. It took seven games, but Phoenix took the series, 4–3.

Basketball fans took a while to warm up to the idea of a Celtics-Suns final. "Some people didn't want us to be there," remembered Phoenix coach John MacLeod. "We were not considered a team with much appeal at the time. They wanted Golden State and Boston in the Finals."

"The most exciting basketball game I've ever seen."
—broadcaster and former star Rick Barry

The first two games served only to validate the naysayers. Boston won by double digits in both games, and it looked as though a four-game sweep was a sure thing. The Suns rallied, though, and played the next two games with the same intensity they had used to beat Golden State. They won Games 3 and 4 to even the series.

Then came Game 5. It was June 4, 1976, and 15,320 exuberant fans filled Boston Garden on this Friday night. The heat was stifling in the arena, and the game didn't begin until 9:00 for television. The fans were wild with anticipation.

The Celtics didn't disappoint them. They jumped out to an early lead. "We were up 22 on them early," said Tommy Heinsohn, Celtics head coach, "but Paul Westphal spun his magic and they came back."

Phoenix cut the Boston lead to 15 by the half and took their first lead of the game with 23 seconds left in regulation. John Havlicek hit one of two free throws for the Celtics with 19

NBA'S GREATEST GAME BY THE NUMBERS
June 4, 1976, at Boston Garden

CELTICS (128)

Player	Min.	FGA	FGM	FTA	FTM	Reb.	Ast.	PF	Pts.
Jim Ard	16	6	3	2	2	1	1	1	8
Dave Cowens	55	23	9	11	8	5	4	6	26
John Havlicek	58	19	8	7	6	5	8	2	22
Steve Kuberski	13	5	2	0	0	3	0	1	4
Glenn McDonald	13	5	3	2	2	0	3	2	8
Don Nelson	20	4	1	2	2	0	1	1	4
Charlie Scott	33	14	3	0	0	2	3	6	6
Paul Silas	44	11	8	1	1	4	4	6	17
Kevin Stacom	3	0	0	0	0	0	0	0	0
Jo Jo White	60	29	15	4	3	0	9	2	33
Totals	**315**	**116**	**52**	**29**	**24**	**20**	**33**	**27**	**128**

SUNS (126)

Player	Min.	FGA	FGM	FTA	FTM	Reb.	Ast.	PF	Pts.
Alvan Adams	37	16	9	2	2	9	5	6	20
Dennis Awtrey	23	3	2	3	3	4	0	6	7
Keith Erickson	4	2	0	0	0	0	1	0	0
Nate Hawthorne	8	3	1	2	2	4	0	3	4
Garfield Heard	61	19	8	2	1	12	4	1	17
Phil Lumpkin	12	2	0	0	0	1	4	0	0
Curtis Perry	52	20	10	4	3	15	6	5	23
Ricky Sobers	41	22	11	4	3	2	6	2	25
Dick Van Arsdale	35	5	1	4	3	4	1	1	5
Paul Westphal	42	20	11	3	3	2	2	4	25
Totals	**315**	**112**	**53**	**24**	**20**	**53**	**29**	**28**	**126**

Score by Periods	1	2	3	4	O1	O2	O3	Total
Celtics	36	25	16	18	6	11	16	128
Suns	18	27	27	23	6	11	14	126

Min. = minutes played; FGA = field goal attempts; FGM = field goals made; FTA = free throws attempted; FTM = free throws made; Reb. = rebounds; Ast. = assists; PF = personal fouls; Pts. =

seconds to go, sending the game into overtime.

The *Phoenix Gazette* would later report that it wasn't a great game until overtime. "The Suns were horrible early in regulation, and the Celtics were horrible late in regulation," said reporter Joe Gilmartin.

The Celtics built a four-point lead twice in the first overtime, and both times the Suns came back. The game went into a second overtime.

As the next five minutes wound down, a Westphal steal led to a jumper by Curtis Perry to give the Suns a one-point lead. Havlicek had time for one more shot, a 15-footer that fans thought gave the Celtics a one-point win at the buzzer. In fact, there was one second remaining.

Mayhem ensued when fans swarmed onto the court. Someone pummeled referee Richie Powers and had to be dragged off. Powers came up from the melee with two fingers in the air, signifying that the game wasn't over. The court was cleared, and the clock was reset to one second.

The Suns were going to have to inbound the ball from behind the Boston basket. Paul Westphal quickly suggested that the Suns call a timeout—one they didn't have. A technical

The heat was never off during the 1976 NBA Finals. When a ball was up for grabs, Boston and Phoenix fought hard.

foul would be called, and the Celtics would get a free throw, but Phoenix would get their inbounds from midcourt, giving them a much better chance to score with so little time on the clock.

Jo Jo White hit the free throw to put Boston up by two. But the Suns had one more chance. Curtis Perry surveyed his options and passed to Gar Heard. From 18 feet out, Heard caught the ball, launching it in a high arch to the hoop. It swished through the net, sending the game into a third overtime. The crowd was stunned.

In spite of the exciting shot that bought them five more minutes, the Suns were unable to hold on for the win. Several starters fouled out, and Glenn McDonald came in for the Celtics. The little-used forward scored six points for Boston, including the final two on a short jumper. Boston won Game 5 at the Garden by a score of 128–126.

The Celtics went on to win Game 6 and the 1976 championship. They will be remembered for winning their 13th NBA title. But it's the Suns who will be remembered for making Game 5 the greatest game ever played—and for the shot "Heard" 'round the world.

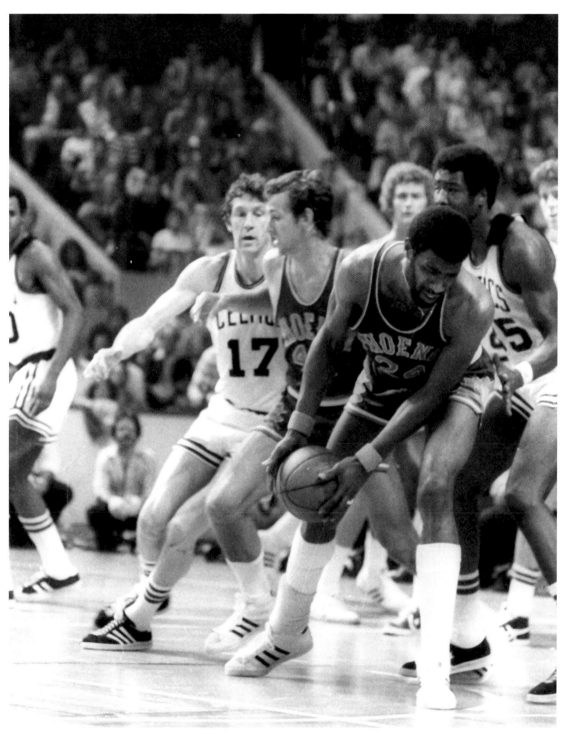

Garfield Heard of Phoenix gets clear with heavy pressure from Boston's John Havlicek (No. 17) and Paul Silas (right) during the first of three overtime periods. Helping is teammate Paul Westphal. The Celtics beat the Suns 128–126.

16

The Fight of the Century

Muhammad Ali was talking. It was standard fare for the motormouthed Louisville
Lip, and you could count on it getting more intense as the final days of the
prefight hype dominated the airwaves. His opponent, current champ Joe Frazier,
was cool with it. He was playing the role of salt-of-the-earth man. But Ali knew he
could get under Frazier's skin if he was vocal enough.

"There ain't but one heavyweight champion of the world—me." That's what Ali said. He'd
been saying it even when he was Cassius Clay, Sonny Liston's challenger in 1963. Clay, he said,
was his "slave name."

The stoic Frazier responded, "No matter what Clay says, I am the defending heavyweight
champion." Frazier loved to call him Clay. Smokin' Joe knew how to raze someone too. The
7-to-5 Vegas odds in favor of Frazier backed him up.

The Garden had been sold out weeks in advance, and each fighter would take home a
guaranteed purse of $2.5 million. With celebrities befitting such a wealthy event all in
attendance, the bell was rung on the opening round of what was to be a classic clash of
pugilistic skill.

The first round saw both fighters exhibit the styles that had made them famous. Ali, the
purer boxer, used quick footwork to move with grace and agility, which gave him the ability to
make full use of his longer reach by attacking the champ with his devastating left jab. Frazier,

however, was relentless in his attack on the midsection of the challenger. Putting his faith in the old boxing adage "Kill the body and the head too will die," Frazier zeroed in on the chiseled physique of his verbose opponent.

In the second, the sellout crowd saw Ali change his approach drastically. Rather than dancing around danger, as he generally did with great success, Ali seemed eager to remain flat-footed and go blow for blow with the shorter Frazier.

At the start of the third round, Ali advanced to the center of the ring before the bell was sounded, seemingly daring the champ to come and get it. During the round, the challenger was admonished by referee Arthur Mercante to keep the chatter down.

> ## "The only thing going through my mind when he got up was what was going through my mind all night: 'Throw punches, just throw punches. Let him do the talking. All I have to do is punch.'"
> —Joe Frazier

The fourth round saw Frazier bloody the nose of Ali, effectively closing the deposed champion's seemingly unstoppable mouth. In the fifth Frazier exhibited some confidence of his own, allowing Ali to give him his best shots while his guard was lowered. The blows of the challenger seemed to do the champ no harm.

The sixth round came and went without giving witness to Ali's prefight prediction for a sixth-round knockout of the defending champion. Frazier continuously pounded Ali's torso with his mighty left hooks, but Ali persevered, and Frazier showed signs of slowing down.

To start the eighth, much of the crowd got behind Ali, and the man who was known for his mouth as well as his fists did not hesitate to point out to the champ who the crowd loved best.

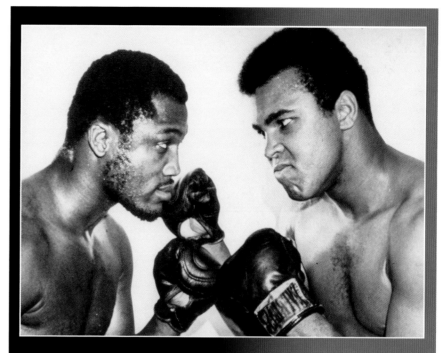

HOW MUHAMMAD ALI LOST THE TITLE
From Louisville to the Nation of Islam

Cassius Clay, now known as Muhammad Ali, has a special place in the sports history of our nation, and with good reason. The finest pugilist of his time, Ali's bravado and confidence held audiences captive for the duration of his career. Love him or hate him, few could resist watching Ali talk his talk and back it up in the ring with his smooth boxing style.

In 1964, Ali had announced he was a member of the Nation of Islam and officially shed the moniker of Cassius Clay. Although the name change was shocking, the nation's growing adoration of the loquacious boxer was hardly slowed by Ali's announcement. However, in 1967, as the United States continued to fight a war in Vietnam, Ali quickly became a villain where he had previously been a hero. He was drafted on April 28, and at the U.S. Armed Forces Examining and Entrance Station in Houston, Texas, Ali made known his intentions to refuse induction into the United States Army. He claimed an exemption from the services on the grounds that he served as a minister for the religion of Islam.

The backlash of Ali's decision was swift and definite. The country recoiled at the thought of their hero refusing to serve his country. The nation, already in racial turmoil, found the issue of Ali's skin color and his refusal to be drafted inseparable. The man who claimed to "float like a butterfly, sting like a bee" was stripped of the heavyweight championship belt he held at the time, sentenced to prison, and fined $10,000. He was released on appeal and spent the next three years of his life clearing his name through the legal system. With his boxing license revoked in most states, Ali remained inactive.

He was granted a New York State boxing license in 1970, and one year later the Supreme Court heard his appeal and ruled in his favor. Ali did eventually earn back the love of boxing fans across the nation, but it was neither instantaneous nor easy. Indeed, given the racial climate of the nation at that time, it is unlikely that any but the Greatest could have made the fans, who were so eager to deride him as a criminal in 1967, chant his name in Madison Square Garden as they did on March 8, 1971.

Invigorated by the support of his admirers, Ali came out strong and took advantage of Frazier's apparent weariness. Using his patented left-right combinations, Ali drove Frazier back but could not land the finishing punch.

All throughout the ninth and tenth rounds Ali went to work with his usual jabs, along with left hooks and short right combinations that battered the face of the heavyweight champion.

Late in the eleventh round the champ made his move. Smokin' Joe came out with a flurry of left hooks and stiff rights that sent the garrulous challenger into the ropes. The twelfth saw Frazier open with a burst of savage blows, then slow the pace to a crawl. Then, without warning, the champ connected with a hammerlike hook that sent Ali sprawling to the canvas.

Muhammad Ali takes a left from Joe Frazier during the 15th round. Frazier won on a unanimous decision and retained his heavyweight title.

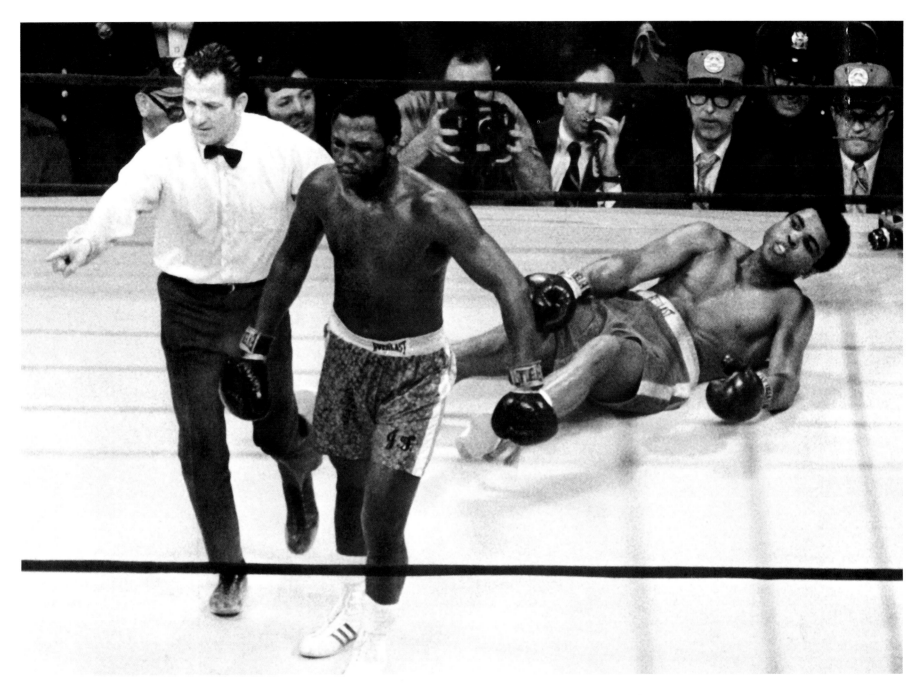

It was this same deadly punch that downed Ali again in the fifteenth and final round of the bout. Incredibly, the two fighters had gone the distance. Along with a bloody nose, Ali's jaw was visibly swollen. Frazier sported one eye swollen nearly shut and a bevy of bruises all over his face. Later Ali would require a trip to the hospital to check for injuries to the ribs made by Frazier's crushing body blows.

The three officials scored the fight 9–6, 11–4, 8–6, all in favor of the defending champion. Joe Frazier, by unanimous decision, had retained the heavyweight title. Fighting against a taller man with a much longer reach, the defending champion had used his fierce will and left hook to walk away from one of the greatest heavyweight fights ever with the belt still around his waist.

Frazier is directed to the ropes by referee Arthur Mercante after knocking down Ali during the 15th round. Frazier won the bout over Ali by decision.

17

Larsen's Perfect Game

Octoher 8, 1956, Yankee Stadium, the Bronx, New York

The 1956 World Series between the New York Yankees and Brooklyn Dodgers was equal parts alley fight and subway series. Sounds like a perfect contest. It was even more perfect, a perfect game—a nine-inning contest in which a pitcher faces 27 batters and none reach base.

The two teams had met in the fall classic no less than seven times in 16 years. In six of those prior rumbles the Yankees had come away victorious. But in 1955 the Dodgers had finally turned the tables, winning four games to three and giving the Bums bragging rights throughout Gotham.

Losing was a foreign concept to most Yankees players and completely unacceptable to their demanding fans. The rivalry was now an all-out turf war, a kind of *West Side Story*, without the dancing.

In the Series opener at Ebbets Field, the Dodgers continued their newfound mastery of the Yanks. With Sal "the Barber" Maglie striking out 10, the Bums rode to a 6–3 victory on the long-ball express, Jackie Robinson and Gil Hodges providing the home-run power.

The Dodgers' dominance reached its apex in Game 2, as the National League champs spotted the Yankees a 6–0 second-inning lead before pummeling them, 13–8. The Yankees starter in that day's embarrassment was Don Larsen. If the Yankees ended up losing the World Series, Larsen would undeniably be the goat.

Larsen's career to date had been distinguished only for its lack of distinction. He had been acquired by the Yankees from Baltimore as part of an 18-player trade in December of 1954. Known as a party animal, he was more renowned for drinking highballs than for throwing fastballs.

In 1955, as a newly minted Yankee, he managed a 9–2 record and a respectable 3.06 ERA. In the 1956 regular season, Larsen posted an 11–5 record and an ERA of 3.26. In short, he had become a dependable, although hardly dominating, major league pitcher. It was not the first time that donning the Yankees

> ## "I think about it every day. Sometimes it's hard to believe it ever happened. I'm glad it did because everybody thinks about that and forgets all the mistakes I made in my career."
> —Don Larsen

pinstripes had transformed a player and salvaged his career, although Larsen's was hardly a phone booth transformation from Clark Kent to Superman—more like Ozzy Osbourne to Ozzie Nelson, from disgrace to respectability.

After the Game 2 debacle, the Yankees, down two games and in full panic mode, returned to the comfort of Yankee Stadium to lick their wounds and prepare for Game 3. It was do-or-die time for the Bronx Bombers, and wily southpaw Whitey Ford was not going to let his team expire on his watch. Ford answered the call with a 5–3 complete-game victory. Buoyed by their success, the rejuvenated Yankees, behind the six-hit pitching of Tom Sturdivant, also won Game 4, 6–2, knotting the World Series at two games apiece.

Despite the two wins, the Yankees could not afford to return to the hostile confines of Ebbets Field teetering on the brink of elimination. Not only must the Yankees win Game 5, they must also rob the feisty Dodgers of their confidence. With sly Sal Maglie once

The feat of pitching a perfect game has been accomplished a total of 16 times in the long history of major league baseball. There was also one game that doesn't qualify by the strictest criteria of "perfect" games. But anyone who witnessed the event, including the opposing team, would be difficult to convince that this was not a perfect effort, at least until one tired infielder made a miscue.

On May 26, 1959, Harvey Haddix of the Pittsburgh Pirates pitched 12 perfect innings of baseball and lost the game to the Milwaukee Braves. On this cold spring evening, he was red hot, retiring 36 consecutive batters in those 12 innings. In the unlucky thirteenth, the streak of perfection ended with an error, an intentional walk, and a double.

As the game entered extra innings, even the Milwaukee fans were cheering for the enemy pitcher to win the game. Lew Burdette was racking up the zeros, too, though the visitors' hits column on the scoreboard climbed into double digits. When the game ended with an error, an intentional walk, and a double, it was as if someone had drawn a mustache on the *Mona Lisa*—a masterpiece had been defaced. The final score was 1–0. The Braves had collected 1 hit, the Pirates 12.

Heroes are supposed to die by a blow from their foe's sword, not one of their own, followed by two more self-inflicted wounds. Felix Mantilla led off the thirteenth by hitting a routine grounder to third baseman Don Hoak. Hoak came up with the ball but threw it into the dirt, allowing Mantilla to reach first safely. The perfect game was no more. The spell was broken. Eddie Matthews sacrificed Mantilla to second base, and Haddix decided to walk the ever-dangerous Hank Aaron in order to set up the double play. With a count of 1–0, the big Braves first baseman Joe Adcock jumped on a hanging slider and hit the ball over the fence. Adcock passed Aaron while rounding the bases and was credited with a double instead of a home run.

Pitchers who have attained baseball perfection are:
- Lee Richmond, Worchester versus Cleveland, 1880
- Monte Ward, Providence versus Boston, 1880
- Cy Young, Boston versus Philadelphia, 1904
- Addie Joss, Cleveland versus Chicago, 1908
- Charley Robertson, Chicago versus Detroit, 1922
- Don Larsen, New York versus Brooklyn, 1956
- Jim Bunning, Philadelphia versus New York, 1964
- Sandy Koufax, Los Angeles versus Chicago, 1965
- Catfish Hunter, Oakland versus Minnesota, 1968
- Len Barker, Cleveland versus Toronto, 1981
- Mike Witt, California versus Texas, 1984
- Tom Browning, Cincinnati versus Los Angeles, 1988
- Dennis Martinez, Montreal versus Los Angeles, 1991
- Kenny Rogers, Texas versus California, 1994
- David Wells, New York versus Minnesota, 1998
- David Cone, New York versus Montreal, 1999

A scoreboard the likes of which was never before seen at a World Series.

again pitching for the Dodgers and the Yankees fortunes placed in the unsteady hands of Don Larsen, confidence was in short supply among Yankees fans and players.

Dodgers batters practically ran to the plate during the final strains of the national anthem to get another crack at Larsen. But the Brooklyn Dodgers were soon to discover that it was a very different Don Larsen from the one they had seen just days earlier. The 6'4", 215-pound right-hander faced leadoff man Junior Gilliam, who had drawn two walks in their previous meeting. Larsen ran the count to 2–2 and then froze the second baseman for called strike three. Pee Wee Reese followed and was also dispatched with his bat still on his shoulder. Duke Snider lined the ball to the right fielder for the third out.

Maglie answered the challenge in the bottom of the first, quickly retiring all three batters, and the battle was on. In the top of the second inning, Jackie Robinson cracked a sharp liner that deflected off third baseman Andy Carey's glove and into the glove of shortstop Gil McDougald, who relayed it to first for the out. Sheer Larsen-y.

Going into the bottom of the fourth inning, there was a perfect row of zeros on the scoreboard. Neither pitcher had surrendered a hit. Mickey Mantle quickly changed that with a single swing of his bat, sending a Maglie delivery into the right-field stands.

The Dodgers responded in the top of the fifth. After Robinson flied out to right, Gil Hodges hit a hard shot to the farthest reaches of the Stadium's vast center field. Mantle, still deserving of the nickname the Commerce Comet, raced toward the fast-dropping ball and, with glove arm fully extended, snared it before it could reach the turf. Larsen's hitless streak remained unbroken.

Following baseball tradition Yankees announcer Mel Allen felt obliged to speak cryptically about the no-hitter. "The Yankees have all the hits in the game," he informed the listening audience. The crowd of 64,519, unrestricted by such baseball protocol, was much less reticent, and murmurs grew to a buzz that increased in intensity as each Dodger returned hitless to the dugout.

The Yankees scored an insurance run in the bottom half of the sixth, and all eyes were now on Larsen. Although he no longer had his crisp fastball, the 27-year-old's toxic mixture of change-ups and curves bamboozled the Dodgers batters.

Larsen's larceny continued in the eighth as he got three key Dodgers: the explosive Jackie Robinson, the clutch Gil Hodges, and the pesky Sandy Amoros. Three outs to go to baseball immortality and perfection.

The ninth inning seemed to many in attendance to unfold in slow motion. Carl Furillo, the brooding but brilliant Dodgers right fielder, was first up. The man they called the Reading Rifle had batted .289 with 21 home runs in 1956. Furillo hit four foul balls before finally flying out to right. One down and two to go. Roy Campanella, who had stroked 20 homers during the regular campaign, stepped into the batter's box. Campy swung at the first offering and drove the ball down the left-field line just foul. A collective intake of air from the crowd, and then the return of the buzz. Campy then grounded out, bringing the crowd to its feet and Larsen to the brink of perfection.

The final batter of the day was Dale Mitchell, pinch hitting for Maglie, who had pitched so brilliantly for the Dodgers. The first pitch was a ball, the second a called strike. The next offering was swung on and missed for strike two. All eyes were on one man—Don Larsen. The next pitch was fouled off, and the count remained at 1–2. The term *perfect tense* now took on a whole new meaning as fans, players, and umpires were in dire need of massage therapy. As Larsen released the next pitch, a fastball, the batter seemed to freeze, and umpire Babe Pinelli called, "Strike three!"

After the game an intrepid reporter, whose grasp of the obvious was obviously slipping, asked Larsen: "Was this the best game you ever pitched?"

Larsen's gem was the turning point of the Series. Although the Dodgers, behind the shutout pitching of Clem Labine, rallied to a 1–0 win the next day in Brooklyn, their bats never fully recovered. In Game 7, the Yanks broke loose on homers by Yogi Berra, Elston Howard, and Moose Skowron. The deflated, demoralized Dodgers managed only three hits and no runs, as the Yankees dismantled the defending champs, 9–0.

Don Larsen had achieved what few mortals can claim: perfection. When the fat lady sang after this performance, she did it like Larsen, with perfect pitch.

At the end of the only perfect World Series game, Yankees catcher Yogi Berra leaps into the arms of Don Larsen, the 27-year-old right-hander from San Diego, California.

18

The Comeback

January 3, 1993, Rich Stadium, Orchard Park, New York

As halftime speeches go, it wasn't exactly R-rated or Knute Rockne material.

The Buffalo Bills trailed the Houston Oilers, 28–3, in the AFC wild-card playoff game, a week after losing the regular-season finale to the same club, 27–3. The Bills' starting quarterback, Jim Kelly, was out with a knee injury, and there seemed little reason for Buffalo coach Marv Levy to get overly excited about what everybody in Rich Stadium expected would be the team's final 30 minutes of the season.

"Whatever happens, you guys have to live with yourselves after today," was Levy's halftime speech. Later he added, "I said it in maybe some stern terms, maybe in a louder voice or very sharply. . . . There was anger in what I said."

But did the coach think his team still had a chance to win? "We had a chance," Levy would say later. "About the same chance a guy has of winning the New York lottery."

Three plays into the second half, the odds of Buffalo making any kind of comeback, even to make the score respectable, had gotten longer. Star running back Thurman Thomas was lost for the rest of the day with a hip injury, and on the next play, quarterback Frank Reich's pass was intercepted by Houston safety Bubba McDowell, who returned it 58 yards for a touchdown. The Bills now trailed, 35–3, with 28 minutes left in the game.

As Reich stood on the sideline, waiting to get back on the field, all he had to do was think back nine years to realize that a comeback of this magnitude was still possible. He had also come off the bench, because of an injury, to play quarterback for Maryland against Miami in the Orange Bowl in 1984. Trailing 31–0, the senior rallied his team to an amazing 42–40 victory, one of the greatest comebacks in college football history.

"Gale Gilbert [the third-string quarterback] came up to me and really encouraged me," Reich said. "He reminded me about it [the Maryland comeback]. He said, 'You did it before in college, there's no reason we can't do it again now.'"

The comeback began innocently enough, with running back Kenneth Davis scoring on a one-yard run. With the Bills trailing 35–10, Levy got daring, figuring he had nothing to lose. He called for an onside kick, and kicker Steve Christie recovered the ball.

"I didn't want to get off the field. I was like, 'Hey, another quarter.' It was that type of situation, that type of adrenaline flowing. You could just see it coming out of people's pores."
—Bills receiver Andre Reed

"I just stuck my head in there. Why not?" Christie said. "Actually, Mark Maddox made the play. He lifted a guy off the ball and I just slid in there and got it. I've got a helmet and shoulder pads. I'm not just a kicker."

Four plays later, Reich hit receiver Don Beebe for a 38-yard touchdown. It was now Houston 35, Buffalo 17.

Said Beebe, "We're on the sidelines and said, 'Hey, obviously we're going to need big plays, but we've just got to make one play at a time and just stay with it. We can score 28, 35 points in this half.' And we just kept making play after play after play, and we kept crawling back into it."

On the Bills' next possession, Reich found wide receiver Andre Reed for a 26-yard scoring pass. In nine minutes, 58 seconds, Buffalo had cut Houston's 32-point lead to 11, 35–24.

The Bills' 32-point comeback victory over the Oilers was not only the greatest comeback in the history of the NFL playoffs, it also was the greatest comeback for a victory in either the playoffs or the regular season.

How they did it:

	1st	2nd	3rd	4th	OT	Total
Houston	7	21	7	3	0	38
Buffalo	3	0	28	7	3	41

Houston—Jeffires 3 pass from Moon (Del Greco kick)
Buffalo—FG Christie 36
Houston—Slaughter 7 pass from Moon (Del Greco kick)
Houston—Duncan 26 pass from Moon (Del Greco kick)
Houston—Jeffires 27 pass from Moon (Del Greco kick)
Houston—McDowell 58 interception return (Del Greco kick)
Buffalo—Davis 1 run (Christie kick)
Buffalo—Beebe 38 pass from Reich (Christie kick)
Buffalo—Reed 26 pass from Reich (Christie kick)
Buffalo—Reed 18 pass from Reich (Christie kick)
Buffalo—Reed 17 pass from Reich (Christie kick)
Houston—FG Del Greco 26
Buffalo—FG Christie 32

Five other great NFL comebacks:

Playoffs
From 24 points, San Francisco 49ers over the New York Giants, 2003
From 20 points, Detroit Lions over San Francisco 49ers, 1957

Regular season
From 28 points, San Francisco 49ers over the New Orleans Saints, 1980
From 26 points, Buffalo Bills over the Indianapolis Colts, 1997
From 25 points, St. Louis Cardinals over the Tampa Bay Bucs, 1987

Houston Oilers kicker Al Del Greco (No. 3) and holder Greg Montgomery (No. 9) juggle the ball after an aborted field-goal attempt during the fourth quarter of the 1993 AFC wild card game.

safety Henry Jones intercepted a Warren Moon pass, returning it 15 yards to the Houston 23.

"In the playoffs, football is a game of attitude," said Buffalo defensive coordinator Walt Corey. "We were letting the Oilers control the tempo of the game [in the first half]. Too many times you talk a better game than you're playing. At halftime, I told them, 'I love you, but if you don't start playing, I'll kill you.'"

After Jones' interception, the Bills gained five yards in three plays, but declined to go for the field goal on fourth-and-five from the 18. Instead, Reich dropped back and found Reed in the end zone with another touchdown pass. The margin was now down to four points, 35–31.

That deficit stood for the next 13 minutes, until Reich again found Reed, this time for a 17-yard scoring pass that capped a seven-play, 74-yard drive. With 3:08 remaining in the game, the Bills had taken their first lead, 38–35.

Houston, who had built their halftime lead on four touchdown passes from Moon, wasn't about to give up now despite their second-half meltdown. Moon directed the Oilers to a 12-play, 63-yard drive, capped by a 26-yard field goal by Al Del Greco with 12 seconds to play, to tie the game, 38–38, and send it into overtime.

The Oilers won the toss, but on the third play from scrimmage, Moon's pass was intercepted by cornerback Nate Odomes. A 15-yard personal foul penalty on Houston's Haywood Jeffires on the return gave the Bills the ball on Houston's 22-yard line. After calling three running plays, Levy sent kicker Christie onto the field.

While waiting for Houston's timeout to expire, Christie said he told himself, "I make

"To tell you the truth, when it's 35–3, you think, 'Let's make it respectable, let's just start generating something; maybe we can get something going,'" Reich said. "That's all I was trying to do."

But after the TD pass to Reed, Reich's attitude changed.

"That's when I knew we had a chance," he said. "It was 35–24 with over a quarter left. The only thing that concerned me was that we were going into the wind in the last quarter."

Reich didn't have much additional time to think about what was happening. The Bills defense was caught up in the comeback effort as well, and on the first play after the kickoff,

The Buffalo Bills bench—including receiver Don Beebe (No. 82) and injured quarterback Jim Kelly (behind Beebe and wearing street clothes)—celebrates Steve Christie's field goal, which put them ahead of the Houston Oilers, 41–38.

Buffalo Bills cornerback Nate Odomes gets a lift from teammate Henry Jones after intercepting a pass by Warren Moon of the Houston Oilers in overtime. That interception set up Christie's game-winning field goal.

these kicks in practice every day. They could have called 10 timeouts and it wouldn't have mattered. I just kept reminding myself to keep it simple, that's how you have to think. I hit it perfect."

Christie's 32-yard field goal completed the greatest comeback in the then 73-year history of the NFL, 41–38, and left the players and coaches on both sides numb.

Reich, who was starting the first playoff game of his career, finished his amazing day by completing 16 of his 22 passes for 230 yards and four touchdowns.

"It's not just devastating, it's embarrassing," Jeffires said. "You see it, but how can you believe it?"

Moon didn't.

"We had control of this game like no one's had control of a game," said Moon. "It's really hard to figure out why. I'm kind of numb by the way everything happened. I'm just trying to figure out why."

For the Bills, the questions of how and why weren't important. All they knew was that they were celebrating, and they were not ready to go home for the winter.

"A couple of times my wife and I have looked at each other and said, 'Did that really happen?'" Reich said 24 hours after the game.

"I look at it as a miracle from God."

19

A Game for the Ages

January 3, 2003, Sun Devil Stadium, Tempe, Arizona

The Ohio State Buckeyes came into the Fiesta Bowl championship series a double-digit underdog to the Miami Hurricanes, a team that had won 34 consecutive games and needed win number 35 to defend its national title.

Those numbers didn't scare the Buckeyes or their fans, who vowed to prove their skeptics wrong and win the school's first championship since 1968. By the fourth quarter, they had earned more than a few believers.

Ohio State took advantage of Miami turnovers and pressured quarterback Ken Dorsey into uncharacteristic mistakes, building a 17–14 lead as the game neared the end of regulation. The Hurricanes, however, were not going to surrender their title that easily.

A 50-yard punt return by wide receiver Roscoe Parrish set up a 40-yard field-goal attempt by Todd Sievers on the final play of the fourth quarter. When his kick was good, the first overtime in the Bowl Championship Series began.

Unlike the sudden-death overtime in professional sports, college football uses a format that gives one team the ball on its opponent's 25-yard line. The team has four chances to move 10 yards and get a first down, just like in regulation. They keep possession either until they fail to make a first down or fail to score. The other team then gets the ball at the 25, and the same procedure is repeated. If both teams score a touchdown or kick a field goal, the game goes to the second overtime to try to determine a winner.

Miami received the ball first and, calling upon the sons of two Hall of Famers, Walter Payton and Kellen Winslow, struck first. Jarrett Payton was filling in for the injured Willis McGahee, Miami's talented running back who suffered two torn ligaments in his knee in the fourth quarter. Payton ran three times for nine yards, then Dorsey hit Kellen Winslow II with a seven-yard scoring pass.

Ohio State took over and quickly found themselves in a big hole—facing a fourth-and-14—to keep their chances alive. Quarterback Craig Krenzel rose to the challenge, hitting Michael Jenkins for a 17-yard gain and a first down.

Moments later, it was fourth-and-3. When Krenzel's pass into the end zone toward Chris Gamble fell incomplete, it appeared the

> ## "I was waiting for the flag, but he kind of hesitated. I didn't see him going for the flag and I thought, 'He ain't going to throw it.' Luckily, he did."
> ### —Ohio State receiver Chris Gamble

Hurricanes had won their second consecutive title. Fiesta Bowl officials began the postgame preparations; Miami players started celebrating. Safety Sean Taylor threw his helmet across the field.

Almost as soon as they began, however, the Hurricanes stopped. Someone noticed the yellow flag lying in the end zone. Field judge Terry Porter had called Miami's Glenn Sharpe for pass interference. The call gave Ohio State the ball at the 1-yard line, and this time Krenzel ran it into the end zone for the tying score that sent the game to a second overtime.

"I didn't see him throw the flag," said Miami coach Larry Coker. "I was on the field, and somebody said, 'Clear the field, the game is not over.' I looked and saw it in the corner of the end zone. I didn't even know when he threw it."

Said Gamble, "He [Sharpe] was holding me. He was in my face mask and my shoulder pads. I was waiting for the flag but he

FROM DIVISION I-AA TO THE FIESTA BOWL: TRESSEL LEADS THE WAY

Jim Tressel of Ohio State became the first coach to lead his team to an NCAA Division I football title in 2002 after earlier having won an NCAA championship at the Division I-AA, Division II, or Division III level.

Tressel was the coach at Youngstown State (Ohio) when it captured the national Division I-AA championship four times, in 1991, 1993, 1994, and 1997.

At 48, Tressel had never led a Division I-A program, but he had 12 winning seasons at Division I-AA. He was 135–57–2 with Youngstown State and previously served as an Ohio State assistant coach, handling quarterbacks and receivers, under Earl Bruce, from 1983 to 1986. He also assisted at Miami of Ohio, Akron, and Syracuse.

Tressel managed to bring gridiron experience and a sense of direction to his new position. Ohio State's reputation as a football powerhouse is a long and storied one. But the Buckeyes took a tumble just before the turn of the millennium and coach John Cooper was fired in early 2001 after Ohio State lost to South Carolina, 24–7, in the Outback Bowl.

Losses were not the only reason cited for the change at the helm. Buckeyes players were also performing poorly in the classroom, taunting opposing teams on the field, and engaging in off-the-field run-ins with the law.

It took only 16 days after Cooper's departure for Ohio State administration to hire Tressel. They were looking for someone to raise academic standards and build team character. Tressel, who was known for his disciplined teams at Youngstown State, was also dedicated to academics, and he was looking to lead a Division I-A team, preferably in Ohio. It was a match made in heaven.

"Having been born in the state of Ohio and idolizing the likes of Paul Brown and Woody Hayes . . . as I sit here and think about . . . following men like that, it's really humbling, and it's so exciting," Tressel said.

It took only a couple of years for Tressel to make his own mark at Ohio State. The 2003 championship win over number one–ranked Miami will go down in the record books as one of the most exciting games ever played.

In two seasons, Tressel definitely turned the team around. He won a national title, and best of all . . . the Buckeyes beat Michigan.

Ohio State running back Maurice Clarett (No. 13) celebrates his overtime touchdown. Clarett's TD gave the Buckeyes a 31–24 win and the championship.

[Porter] kind of hesitated. I didn't see him going for the flag and I thought, 'He ain't going to throw it.' Luckily he did and I'm like 'whew.'"

Porter's explanation for the delay was that he wanted to make certain he had the call correct.

"I saw the guy holding the guy prior to the ball being in the air," Porter said. "He was still holding him, pulling him down while the ball was in the air."

Ohio State got first possession in the second overtime and scored on freshman Maurice

Clarett's five-yard run. Now Miami needed a touchdown to tie and set up a third overtime.

The Hurricanes moved the ball to the 1-yard line, facing a fourth down. Dorsey, who had been knocked out of the game for one play, dropped back to pass. Ohio State linebacker Cie Grant blitzed and forced Dorsey to unload the ball. The pass fell incomplete, and this time there were no flags. Ohio State was the national champion.

"I can't describe it," said Buckeyes linebacker Matt Wilhelm. "You can use

whatever joyous word you want—*amazing*, *incredible*, *fantastic*—it's all of those things and more."

The result left Miami players in tears. Some on their sideline, including Coker, had never lost a Miami game before.

"The loss, without question, was devastating," Coker said, "especially when you're down, come back and have a chance to win, think you have it won, and then you don't. It's one of those things that will take a long time to get over. You may never get over it."

Ohio State coach Jim Tressel obviously did not want to get over the way the final result made him feel.

"This was two great heavyweights slugging it out," he said. "We knew if we did the things we needed to do, we would compete."

Krenzel, not the more heralded Dorsey, was the game's offensive MVP, leading all rushers with 81 yards and directing the two touchdown drives in overtime.

"All I know is he did for us what we needed done," Tressel said. "He led the team, fought like crazy. He made plays, especially when they had to be made."

Ohio State safety Donnie Nickey said the Buckeyes always believed they could win, even if they didn't always have a lot of support.

"We never panic, never give up, no surrender all season," Nickey said. "We knew we had the heart to take this thing home, and we did it."

Miami defender Glenn Sharpe (right) hits Ohio State receiver Chris Gamble in the end zone during overtime in the 2003 Fiesta Bowl in Tempe, Arizona. Sharpe was called for pass interference, giving Ohio State the chance to score and continue the overtime.

20

The Long Count
September 25, 1927, Soldier Field, Chicago

J ack Dempsey and Gene Tunney could not possibly have been more different. Tunne
was a well-read gentleman and as pure a boxer as they come. He was a classic
counterfighter; he always seemed to be thinking two punches ahead of his
opponent. Dempsey was nothing of the sort. He had spent years living as a hobo in
the American West, getting his knuckles bloody in the saloon brawls that were so common
in the early part of the 20th century. He was a brawler through and through and had spent
his seven years as champion proving that he could bring destruction to opponents with
either his right or his left, both of which were constantly flying during a match.

These two men had first met in the ring a year before during a driving rainstorm in
Philadelphia, and Tunney had left no doubts that he was indeed the superior boxer. He had
allowed the overaggressive Dempsey to tire himself throwing combinations that did not
connect, and had scored enough of his own points to cruise to a 10-round decision.

The rematch was a national event, and the proceeds from the gate set a new world
record at $2.65 million. More than 104,000 spectators packed into the stadium to witness
Tunney's second defense of his heavyweight championship against the man who had held it,
and the nation's attention, for so long.

The bout started with the ever-charging Dempsey taking the offensive against the wily
champion. Tunney let Dempsey charge but never let him get too close for too long. Throughout

the early rounds Tunney chose his spots wisely and allowed the challenger to expend huge amounts of energy without doing much damage. It was clear to all involved that despite Dempsey's more rigorous preparation, the ex-champ was not the quick and brutally strong pugilist he had been three years earlier.

And then, with 50 seconds having gone by in the seventh round of this somewhat lopsided match, the old Dempsey showed through for just a moment. Dempsey, tired but still attacking, threw a solid right that landed square in the face of the champ.

> ## "It appeared they gave Tunney a generous count in the seventh—just enough extra time to let him get his bearings and climb back on his bicycle. Gus Wilson's watch ticked off 15 seconds while Tunney was on the floor and Gus, as a trainer for many fighters, has been in the business long enough to be able to read a stopwatch."
>
> —Jack Dempsey

He followed with a devastating left hook that found Tunney's chin. Yet another right had the champion stumbling backward into the ropes, and as Tunney bounced back toward his suddenly dangerous challenger, another hook awaited his exposed jaw.

Tunney, unthinkably, began to fall. Dempsey was on fire, and the carnage was not yet over. As the champion fell, Dempsey let loose with a four-punch barrage that hastened Tunney's journey to the canvas. The roar of the crowd was such that nothing else was audible. Tunney hit the floor, and the fans were on their feet, thinking that they had seen the final annihilation by the slugging ex-champ.

Jack Dempsey was on the short end of the longest knockdown count in the history of professional boxing was born in Manassa, Colorado, on June 24, 1895. Having no plans to become one of the most well-known pugilists in boxing history, he began his fighting career as a transient miner who got his start using the name Kid Blackie in the saloons of Colorado mining towns. According to legend, Dempsey did not lose a single fight while taking on all comers.

It didn't take him long to find the national stage. In 1916, Dempsey headed for New York to try his luck as a professional. Using raw power, blinding speed, and excellent agility, the 6', 190-pound Dempsey began to turn the heads of boxing fans everywhere, depositing savage blows upon the heads of his opponents.

Dempsey gained the heavyweight title of the world in 1919 when he used his devastating left hook to defeat Jess Willard. From that point on, the Manassa Mauler became a household name and a bona fide sports star. Perhaps his most savage fight came in his 1923 title defense against Luis Firpo. Dempsey knocked Firpo down an astonishing seven times over the first two minutes of the first round. Firpo then regrouped and sent Dempsey flying through the ropes and out of the ring. Although dazed, Dempsey survived the round and proceeded to knock Firpo out in the second round.

Despite losing the heavyweight title to Gene Tunney in 1926 and failing to recapture it in their 1927 rematch, Dempsey remained one of boxing's biggest stars well into the thirties, boxing in exhibitions. He retired in 1940 with a record of 69–6–9 with 49 of his victories coming by knockout. The brawny fighter died May 31, 1983.

They were wrong. Dempsey, as was his tradition, remained standing over Tunney when the champ hit the mat. However, according to the Illinois State Athletic Commission, in the event of a knockdown the opponent must retreat to the farthest neutral corner before the referee begins to count the man down. Apparently not realizing this rule, when referee Dave Barry motioned for him to go to the neutral corner, Dempsey declined.

Gene Tunney, the champ, was a well-read gentleman and as pure a boxer as they come.

Meanwhile, Tunney remained down. Barry proceeded to attempt to move Dempsey in the proper direction, and finally began his count at one. Meanwhile, the timekeeper had already reached a count of five. At Barry's count of three, Tunney lifted his head for the first time, a full eight seconds after he had met the canvas. It was not until Barry had reached a count of nine, 14 seconds after he was first knocked down, that the defending champion rose.

But rise he did, and the "Long Count" had found its place in the annals of great sports controversies.

Tunney unscrambled his brain quickly enough to outbox Dempsey for the next three rounds, and he took the decision in similar fashion to his first victory over Dempsey in Philadelphia.

Later Tunney claimed that he would have gotten up in time to beat the 10-second count even if Barry had picked up the timekeeper's count. However, he admitted to not remembering the argument between Barry and Dempsey that ensued after the knockdown. Furthermore, the champ only defended his title once more before joining Rocky Marciano as the only heavyweight champions to ever retire as champs and remain retired. Lennox Lewis may join this group if he does not at some point return to the ring.

For Dempsey the brawler, Chicago was the last time he stepped into the ring. Both fighters had given everything in their two meetings, and there could not have been a more fitting way for two of boxing's greatest careers to end than with one of the most controversial fights in the history of the sport.

Referee Dave Barry delivers the count over
downed champion Tunney as challenger
Jack Dempsey stands in the corner (at left)
during their heavyweight title rematch at
Soldier Field in Chicago. Tunney got up at
nine and went on to win the championship.

Third Team

21

The Catch
January 10, 1982, Candlestick Park, San Francisco

As the San Francisco 49ers offense trotted onto the field, they didn't look at the clock or the scoreboard. They didn't worry about the score of the NFC championship game, which showed that they were losing to the Dallas Cowboys, 27–21. They didn't worry about the time remaining in the game, four minutes and 54 seconds.

All they saw was an 89-yard patch of grass between them and the end zone.

"I looked down the field and I saw that patch of grass between our huddle and their goal posts," San Francisco center Fred Quillan told *Sports Illustrated*. "I thought, 'That's it. That one patch of grass between us and the Super Bowl.'"

There also were 11 Dallas defenders whose goal was to keep the 49ers out of the end zone, thus assuring their own trip to the Super Bowl. The Cowboys had frustrated third-year quarterback Joe Montana all game, forcing him to throw three interceptions and sacking him three times, and they didn't show any signs that they were going to stop pressuring him now.

The drive began unspectacularly as Montana's first pass fell incomplete. Next came a draw play to Lenvil Elliott, which gained six yards, setting up a third-and-4. The call was a sideline pass to Freddie Solomon, who hauled in the low throw from Montana, good for a six-yard gain and a drive-saving first down.

> ## "It was a spectacular throw, made under duress. It was thrown exactly where it needed to be thrown."
> ### —49ers receiver Dwight Clark

Two running plays followed, sweeps in opposite directions, which were good for a combined 18 yards. An incomplete pass might have stalled the drive, but before the 49ers had to make another third-down conversion, the Cowboys were hit with an offside call that gave San Francisco a first down. A five-yard pass to fullback Earl Cooper moved the 49ers into Dallas territory just as the two-minute warning sounded.

A reverse to Solomon picked up 14 yards, and Montana went back to the air, threading a 10-yard pass to Dwight Clark that Dallas defender Everson Walls almost knocked down.

A 12-yard gain on another pass to Solomon moved the ball to the Dallas 13 as the 49ers called timeout with 1:15 to play. Both teams were weary, some players were throwing up, and others could barely stand.

"I looked over at them," said 49ers guard Randy Cross. "They had, well, I don't want to say a beaten look, but I saw on their faces the same look Thomas Hearns had when Sugar Ray hit him a few times. They had had us backed up, but now they were no longer the aggressors. They were fighting for their lives."

Another sweep by Elliott was good for a seven-yard gain to the Dallas 6. Timeout, San Francisco, 58 seconds to go.

Run or pass? The 49ers had time for either, but 49ers coach Bill Walsh decided to put the ball in the air and called for a pass designed for Solomon but with Clark a secondary receiver in the back of the end zone. A scrambling Montana, avoiding the Dallas rush, didn't get a clear look at Clark but knew from experience where the receiver would be. He let the ball go.

Montana got hit and knocked to the ground. Clark saw the ball coming toward him, only too high.

"It was over my head," said the 6'4" Clark. "I thought, 'oh, oh, I can't go that high.' Something got me up there. It must have been God or something."

Clark came down with the ball, and "the Catch" became a part of pro football lore. The touchdown tied the game, and Ray Wersching's extra point gave the 49ers the lead with 51 seconds to play. San Francisco's Jim Stuckey recovered a Dallas fumble moments later to complete the storybook ending.

Cowboy safety Charlie Waters saw it happening, but he still couldn't believe it.

"We should have stopped them on that last drive," Waters said. "We stopped them pretty good most of the game. But that last drive, for some reason, was unstoppable."

San Francisco quarterback Joe Montana looks for an open receiver during the 1982 NFC championship game.

Dwight Clark leaps high to gather in a Montana pass that tied the game late in the fourth quarter.

22

The Drive

January 11, 1987, Cleveland Stadium, Cleveland

When Brian Brennan caught the pass from Bernie Kosar and turned it into a 48-yard touchdown with 5:43 to play in the AFC championship game, there was every reason to believe that the Cleveland Browns were headed to Super Bowl XXI.

The touchdown gave the Browns a 20–13 lead over the Denver Broncos, and when the following kickoff was misplayed and finally downed, the ball was on Denver's own 2-yard line. Nobody in Cleveland Stadium believed the Broncos—going against the wind, intermittent snow, and a five-degree windchill—had a chance of scoring the tying touchdown.

Except John Elway.

"In the huddle after that kickoff to the 2, he smiled," said Denver wide receiver Steve Watson. "I couldn't believe it. And he said, 'If you work hard, good things are going to happen.' And then he smiled again."

Only two plays into the drive, however, the odds against Denver's comeback had only increased. It was third-and-2 on the 10-yard line as the Broncos called timeout. Coach Dan Reeves told Elway to hand the ball off to Sammy Winder, who went over left guard for a 2-yard gain and a first down.

> **"I suddenly flashed on something I was thinking about before the game. Great quarterbacks make great plays in great games. That's what it's all about, isn't it?"**
>
> —John Elway

The drive was alive, and Elway was warming up. On second-and-7, he scrambled for an 11-yard gain and another first down.

Elway then found Steve Sewell open for a 22-yard gain and hit Watson for a 12-yard gain, moving the ball to the Cleveland 40 with 1:59 to play. The Cleveland fans kept rooting on both the Browns' defense and the clock. The defense roared first, following an incomplete pass, by sacking Elway for an eight-yard loss.

The Broncos called timeout. It was third-and-18. On the sideline, Reeves told Elway to try to pick up half of the needed yardage, knowing they would still have a fourth down to play.

Instead, Elway found Mark Jackson open for a 20-yard gain and a first down at the Cleveland 28.

A 14-yard pass to Sewell on second down moved the ball to the 14, and then Elway scrambled again, picking up nine yards to move the ball to the 5. The clock wasn't moving fast enough to please the Browns faithful, who suddenly thought the clock had a better chance of stopping Elway than the Browns.

With 37 seconds remaining, Elway again found Jackson, this time for the touchdown that most people thought was impossible. Rich Karlis' extra point tied the game and sent it to overtime.

On the 98-yard drive, Elway completed six of nine passes, including two incompletions deliberately thrown out of bounds, for 78 yards, and ran for 20.

"Being human, you tend to doubt yourself at times," said wide receiver Vance Johnson. "But John never seemed to doubt anything at the end. Very seldom have I seen him that calm."

Even when the Browns won the coin toss to begin the overtime, everybody in the stadium knew if Elway and the Broncos got the ball back again, the odds were definitely in their favor.

The Denver defense did its part, stopping the Browns on their first possession and forcing a punt. Elway and the Broncos' offense returned to the field with the ball on their 25.

Elway moved the ball to midfield, where he faced a third-and-12. No problem. He found Watson for a 28-yard gain. After three running plays by Winder designed to get the ball into the middle of the field, Karlis came on to try the winning field goal.

"I tried to take the pressure off myself," Karlis said. "John said, 'It's like practice,' and I thought about it and said, 'Yeah, it's just another kick.'"

Karlis did pull the ball slightly, but the 33-yard kick was good enough for the Broncos to move on to the Super Bowl.

"You know how you'll think the night before about how you'd like to do great things in the game?" Elway said. "Well, this is the kind of game you dream about."

Denver Broncos place kicker Rich Karlis (above) follows through on the overtime field goal that gave them a 23–20 victory. Holding is Gary Kubiak.

Denver Broncos quarterback John Elway (No. 7) eludes Cleveland Browns defender Reggie Camp as he scrambles out of the pocket near the end zone. Denver scored during this series of downs.

23

Nicklaus' Sixth Green Jacket

April 10–13, 1986, Augusta National Golf Club, Georgia

When sportswriters and oddsmakers compiled their lists of the top contenders for the 1986 Masters, one name was conspicuously absent: Jack Nicklaus. At 46, the five-time Masters champion was considered past his prime, particularly in comparison to such top-notch players as Seve Ballesteros, Greg Norman, Tom Watson, and defending Masters champion Bernhard Langer. Once the face of professional golf, Nicklaus had not won a major tournament since 1980. Now, six years later, the Golden Bear was regarded as a dark horse contender at Augusta. In fact, some sportswriters had gone so far as to suggest that Nicklaus was basically finished.

But Nicklaus wasn't ready to join the Senior Tour just yet, no matter what the sportswriters were saying about his chances for victory. Turning a deaf ear to these dire assessments of his chances, Nicklaus defied the odds to emerge victorious in a tournament that is still talked about in golf circles today.

There's an old adage that The Masters doesn't really start until the back nine on Sunday. Such was the case for Nicklaus, whose solid playing put him in fifth place at 2 under par after 54 holes. At that point, Norman topped the standings at 6 under par, with Ballesteros, Langer, and Nick Price close behind at 5 under.

> "[One writer] said I was dead, washed up, through, with no chance whatsoever to win again. I was sizzling. I kept thinking, 'Dead, huh? Washed up, huh?' "
>
> —Jack Nicklaus

As the final day wore on, however, the attention began to shift to Nicklaus, whose birdies on the tenth and eleventh holes put him at 5 under. The crowd responded enthusiastically; from that moment, it became clear that the "old-timer" was far from finished. Even the commentators, who had virtually ignored Nicklaus throughout the tournament, began to regard Nicklaus as a bona fide contender for an unprecedented sixth Masters title.

While Nicklaus soared, others, such as Norman and Tom Kite, began to stumble. Norman's double bogey on the tenth hole cost him the lead. And Kite, who had earlier made eagle on the par-5 eighth, missed the green on the twelfth hole. Cheered on by the gallery, Nicklaus continued his steady climb to the top spot, then held by Ballesteros at 7 under par.

After Ballesteros hit into the water on fifteen and took a bogey, Nicklaus pulled ahead of the pack with another birdie on seventeen. It had been 11 years since he had topped the standings by himself in The Masters final round. At the eighteenth hole, however, trouble loomed when his approach landed 40 feet short of the hole. Nicklaus putted the ball to within a foot and a half and tapped in for a final-round 65 and a total of 279, 9 under par. Elated, Nicklaus embraced his caddie, son Jack Jr., signed his scorecard, and headed to the clubhouse to watch the remaining players.

One by one, they dropped out of contention: Ballesteros, Langer, and

Watson. Soon, only Kite and Norman stood between Nicklaus and his sixth green jacket. But Kite missed a 12-foot birdie putt on eighteen and Norman finished with a bogey—both having squandered a chance at a playoff.

With this victory, Jack Nicklaus spectacularly proved his naysayers wrong. It was to be the Golden Bear's last hurrah at The Masters. Four years later, he joined the Senior Tour after racking up an incredible 71 victories on the PGA Tour, including 18 Grand Slam titles. Of all his victories, the 1986 Masters still has the most resonance for Nicklaus, who has called it "my greatest moment in golf."

THE 1986 MASTERS TOURNAMENT
Final Standings—Top Players

Rank	Player	R1	R2	R3	R4	Total	Par	Money
1	Jack Nicklaus	74	71	69	65	279	-9	$144,000
2T	Greg Norman	70	72	68	70	280	-8	$70,400
2T	Tom Kite	70	74	68	68	280	-8	$70,400
4	Seve Ballesteros	71	68	72	70	281	-7	$38,400
5	Nick Price	79	69	63	71	282	-6	$32,000
6T	Jay Haas	76	69	71	67	283	-5	$27,800
6T	Tom Watson	70	74	68	71	283	-5	$27,800
8T	Tommy Nakajima	70	71	71	72	284	-4	$23,200
8T	Payne Stewart	75	71	69	69	284	-4	$23,200
8T	Bob Tway	70	73	71	70	284	-4	$23,200
11T	Donnie Hammond	73	71	67	74	285	-3	$16,960
11T	Sandy Lyle	76	70	68	71	285	-3	$16,960
11T	Mark McCumber	76	67	71	71	285	-3	$16,960
11T	Corey Pavin	71	72	71	71	285	-3	$16,960
11T	Calvin Peete	75	71	69	70	285	-3	$16,960

Jack Nicklaus (left) watches his shot go for a birdie on the seventeenth at The Masters. The shot gave him the lead and his sixth green jacket.

Nicklaus reacts as he finishes on the eighteenth to win The Masters.

24

Lorenzo's Dunk

April 4, 1983, University Arena (the Pit), Albuquerque, New Mexico

When Dereck Whittenburg's desperation shot went up, Jim Valvano's reaction was the same as everybody else in the crowd at the NCAA championship game. He could tell the shot was going to be short, and he thought his North Carolina State Wolfpack was going to overtime against Houston.

What Valvano didn't see was that Lorenzo Charles had also realized the shot was going to be short and was in position for the rebound and put-back. That's exactly what he did, slamming a dunk as time ran out to give N.C. State the 54–52 victory and the national title.

"They almost stole the ball on us, but then Dereck got off the shot and Lorenzo banged it in," Valvano said. "You need luck in a national tournament. Being in the right place at the right time is going to help you win a close game. Fortunately, we got the Hail Mary shot in the right spot."

The win capped a comeback from a six-point deficit in the game's final three minutes against the top-ranked Cougars, led by center Hakeem Olajuwon.

Houston's strategy of turning to a delay game with 10 minutes to go backfired.

"I did it because I had confidence in our offense," said Houston coach Guy Lewis. "I thought we could pull them out for layups, but we got only one."

> "When that shot left Dereck's hand, I could see it was short. All of a sudden Lorenzo grabs it and dunks it. At that moment, what did I know? Two things: I have the ring, and 50 million people are watching."
>
> —North Carolina State coach Jim Valvano

The other key to the Wolfpack's comeback was missed free throws, a problem Houston had struggled with all year.

Michael Young missed the front end of a one-and-one with 2:55 to play, with Houston ahead 52–48. A 24-foot basket by Whittenburg with two minutes to go

tied the game at 52, and then with 1:05 to go, Houston's Alvin Franklin also missed the first of a one-and-one chance and N.C. State grabbed the rebound.

"Really, and truly, what was predicted about us all year came true," Lewis said, "that we'd miss free throws in a big game and lose."

Following Franklin's miss, N.C. State called timeout with 44 seconds to play. They eventually worked the ball to Whittenburg, but only after Houston's Benny Anders almost intercepted a pass. Whittenburg recovered, and unsure of how much time was left, launched his shot.

"I was looking up, trying to find the clock," Whittenburg said. "I couldn't find it. I didn't want to hold the ball as time ran out. So the only thing I thought of was to get it up at the basket. When I shot it, I was looking at it to go in, and then I saw Lorenzo dunk it and time run out."

The victory touched off a mad celebration as Valvano roared off the bench, trying to grab and hug anybody he could find.

"It's a dream," Valvano said. "That's what I told the players at halftime, that they were 20 minutes away from the dream. I had the dream for 16 years as a coach, and they had it all their years in college."

The tempo of the game and N.C. State's tough defense gave the Wolfpack the chance to win the game against the heavily favored Cougars, who had won 26 games in a row.

"It was billed as a game of tempo, and that's what it was," Lewis said. "They made us shoot the worst we did all year. We still got enough shots to win the game, but we missed a lot of easy shots."

For Valvano, the only thing that mattered was the last shot, which went in. "The great thing about college basketball is that the national title is decided on the floor, not in the polls," he said. "There's always hope. If we don't beat Wake Forest, 71–70, we don't play in the NCAA tourney. Is that a great story?"

North Carolina State sophomore forward Lorenzo Charles dunks the ball for a 54-52 win.

Hakeem Olajuwon brings down a rebound for Houston during the 1983 NCAA championship game in Albuquerque. Looking on is North Carolina State's Cozell McQueen.

ALL THAT COUNTS IS THE WIN

En route to the 1983 NCAA championship, the North Carolina State Wolfpack won several close games to put themselves in position for the NCAA title.

In fact, it wasn't until season's end that North Carolina State's record improved to 17 and 10. Their regular-season performance was so mediocre that the Wolfpack needed a couple of strong wins or an unlikely ACC championship to earn an invitation to join the Big Dance.

In the ACC tournament's first round, N.C. State trailed Wake Forest by seven points with nine minutes to play, winning on a free throw by Lorenzo Charles with three seconds left.

In the next game, the Wolfpack trailed North Carolina by six points in overtime before rallying for a 91–84 victory.

Finally, in the ACC title game, N.C. State beat fourth-ranked Virginia, 81–78, on Dereck Whittenburg's two free throws with seconds to play.

Close calls continued as the Wolfpack rolled through the NCAA Tournament.

In the West Regional, N.C. State trailed Pepperdine by five points with 57 seconds left in overtime. The Wolfpack tied it on a basket with six seconds left, then won in the second overtime.

In the second round, Nevada–Las Vegas led N.C. State by 12 points in the second half before State won, 71–70, on a basket with four seconds to play.

And in a rematch against Virginia in the West Regional Finals, N.C. State trailed by seven points with 10 minutes to go. The Wolfpack won, 63–62 on Charles' two free throws with 22 seconds left. Virginia missed two shots at the buzzer.

25

Slaughter's Mad Dash

October 15, 1946, Sportsman's Park, St. Louis

For each triumphal moment in baseball, there is often a hero, but just as often there is also a goat. Sometimes it depends on perspective. Red Sox fans have lived for more than 50 years with the bitter gripe, "Pesky held the ball!" Worse, so has Johnny Pesky. The accusation is in reference to a decisive play in Game 7 of the 1946 World Series, when some judged that Sox shortstop Johnny Pesky hadn't relayed the ball quickly enough from center field to home plate, thereby allowing Enos Slaughter to score what proved to be the game-winning run. In St. Louis, though, they don't talk about Pesky. Cardinals fans give credit instead to Country Slaughter for making a "mad dash" from first base all the way around to home on a hit that truly was just a single.

Harry "the Hat" Walker—whom Pesky would coach with Pittsburgh more than a decade later—was the hitter. It was the bottom of the eighth. Boston had scored first with one run in the top of the first, but St. Louis came back with one in the second and two more in the fifth.

Dramatically, the Red Sox tied the game in the top of the eighth when Dom DiMaggio doubled off the right-center-field screen, driving in the two pinch-hitters who had preceded him. DiMaggio injured himself, forcing him to come out of the game.

> ## "I didn't know it was anything special because I play every game the same way—to win."
> —Cardinals outfielder Enos Slaughter

Replacing DiMaggio in center field was Leon Culberson. Had DiMaggio been in center, the outcome of the game might well have been different.

In the bottom of the frame, Slaughter singled, but reliever Bob Klinger got the next two batters out, the first on a botched sacrifice bunt he caught while running toward the first-base line, and the second on a fly to Ted Williams in left. Slaughter decided to get aggressive on the base paths and try to make something happen. The right-handed Klinger wound up, and Slaughter was off and running for second before Klinger had even released the pitch. He was a third of the way there by the time the ball reached the plate. Walker, a .237 hitter in 1946, hit the ball sharply to left-center. Slaughter rounded the bag and headed to third. The ball wasn't hit that deep, but it was perfectly positioned; Culberson ran over to field it, angling a bit deeper in the process.

No one would have expected Slaughter to try to score, yet he was almost to third by the time the Sox center fielder got to the ball. The proper play was to throw to Pesky, the cutoff man, who moved out to the edge of the infield grass to take Culberson's throw. Pesky was then expected to look to second base and run the ball back in to hold Walker to a single while Slaughter pulled up at third. There didn't seem to be anything unusual about the play and, with no particular urgency and without any hesitation, Culberson lofted the ball to Pesky. Pesky took the throw and looked toward second, but then he saw Slaughter making his "mad dash" to the plate. Surprised, Pesky geared up and threw home. A perfect bullet might yet have had Slaughter, but Slaughter was really too close to the plate, and Johnny's throw went about eight feet up the line. Meanwhile, Walker took second base.

The Cardinals had taken a 4–3 lead, one which they held in the ninth, despite a threat from the Sox as both Rudy York and Bobby Doerr singled to lead off the inning. Harry Brecheen shut down the Sox, however, and earned his third victory of the Series.

Rival World Series managers Joe Cronin of the Red Sox (left) and Eddie Dyer of the Cardinals shake hands.

YOU MAKE THE CALL

"Pesky held the ball!" For more than 50 years that phrase has stuck in the minds (and the craw) of New Englanders. If only it could have been caught on film. But it was! Two different films of the play exist, and neither shows any clear hesitation on Pesky's part, although some might interpret a slight hitch in his throw.

None of the principals involved faulted Pesky. If anyone might be to blame for the goat horns affixed to him, it may well have been Johnny himself, as disconsolate as anyone with the loss of the game and the Series. The press reaction was more mixed than player reaction, but hardly conclusive. In 1962 the *Boston American*'s Huck Finnegan wrote, "Instead of looking for a goat, however, it would have been wiser simply to credit Slaughter with a daring and imaginative piece of base running."

St. Louis sportswriter Bob Broeg was there, and he feels the same way: it was Slaughter's "mad dash," his daring, and his speed that merit attention, not Pesky's play. "I didn't sense any hesitation. It was a run and hit and Slaughter was running. It was a slicing fly ball and [if he hadn't been replaced] DiMaggio maybe would have caught the ball! As he hit second base, he said to himself, 'I'm going to score!' Pesky was surprised and off balance, his throw was weak and (as it happened) late, but he did not hold the ball." Broeg remains upset to this day that the official scorers—there were three of them, this being the World Series—scored Walker's looping fly ball in front of Culberson a double. A rookie reporter at the time, Broeg says he told the scorers then and there, "Gentlemen, you know what? By scoring this a double, you've taken the romance out of a great run!" Broeg told this author, "I'm very sensitive about that, because it's not fair to Pesky and it's not fair to Slaughter." In his book *Bob Broeg: Memories of a Hall of Fame Sportswriter*, Broeg wrote, "I always resented that, arbitrarily, unfairly, and unromantically, the official scorers called Walker's game-winning hit a double. . . . Harry . . . agreed it was a single, not a double, as I insisted to the official scorers. They didn't listen. Too bad. Heck, wouldn't history treat the Paul Revere ride of Enos Slaughter more dramatically if, as most certainly happened, the big-butted buzzard from Carolina scored the winning run from first base on a SINGLE!"

26

Watson's Birdie Chip

June 20, 1982, Pebble Beach, California

Tom Watson was in trouble. In the final round of the 1982 U.S. Open at Pebble Beach, his seventeenth-hole tee shot had landed with an ominous thud in the rough between two bunkers, 18 feet from the green.

The odds of defeating longtime rival Jack Nicklaus now appeared slight, if not downright impossible. Unless Watson could pull off a miraculous chip shot, he would have to settle for a second-place finish in his 11th attempt to win his first U.S. Open title.

The 1982 U.S. Open was merely the latest chapter in the Nicklaus-Watson rivalry. Five years earlier, Watson had beaten Nicklaus in the 1977 Masters with a birdie on the seventeenth hole.

History had repeated itself later that same year in the British Open, when Watson had again narrowly defeated Nicklaus with *another* seventeenth-hole birdie.

Today, at the Pebble Beach Golf Links overlooking Carmel Bay, it appeared that Nicklaus would prevail.

In the early rounds of the tournament, however, neither player had taken the lead. That honor belonged to veteran Bruce Devlin, who broke out of the pack with a 36-hole total of 139. The 44-year-old Devlin, who had not won a tournament in 10 years, was on his way to becoming the oldest U.S. Open winner

> ## "Ever since I was 10 years old I had dreamed of winning this title."
> ### —Tom Watson

in history—until a couple of ill-timed bogeys took him out of the running.

Defending champion David Graham also fell by the wayside after double-bogeying the thirteenth hole in the final round.

While more and more players faded, Nicklaus played a spectacular final round, with six birdies to his credit. In contrast, Watson alternately birdied and bogeyed through holes eleven to sixteen toward

the seventeenth-hole showdown with Nicklaus.

At the seventeenth hole, Watson turned to his caddie, Bruce Edwards, who handed him a sand wedge to make the chip shot. "Get it close," Edwards said.

The seventeenth hole at Pebble Beach is an infamous par 3. According to Bill Rogers, the 1981 British Open champion, "A man could drop the ball on the edge of the seventeenth green with his hand and it wouldn't stop short of the cup, so fast was the green." But Watson had been preparing for this moment for years.

"I've practiced that shot for hours, days, months, and years," he said in a later interview. "It's a shot you have to know if you're going to do well in the Open, where there's high grass around the green."

Already in the clubhouse after shooting par on both the seventeenth and eighteenth holes, Nicklaus watched his rival on the monitor. Nicklaus had finished the fourth round with a score of 69, which set his final score at 284. Two years earlier, he had set a tournament record with a final score of 272 and won his fourth U.S.

Open title. Watson's unfortunate tee shot at the seventeenth hole had put a fifth U.S. Open title within Nicklaus' grasp.

Watson made the chip shot. The ball rose gracefully from the rough and landed on the green. As it rolled toward the hole, Watson stood there, tense with anticipation, until it became clear that he had pulled off the impossible. The crowd roared and Watson ran onto the green, arms raised in triumph.

Back in the clubhouse, Nicklaus watched his chances for victory fade as Watson's miraculous chip shot gave him a one-stroke lead. Once the excitement subsided, Watson went on to birdie the eighteenth hole and finish the tournament with a winning score of 282. Gracious in defeat, Nicklaus emerged from the clubhouse to congratulate Watson. As he shook Watson's hand, Nicklaus smiled and said with a twinkle in his eye, "You little son of a bitch, you're something else."

In the annals of professional golf, Watson's remarkable chip shot has taken its place alongside Gene Sarazen's double eagle at the 1935 Masters as one of the all-time great shots. Although Watson ultimately won 39 PGA Tournaments and was named the PGA's Player of the Year six times, the 1982 U.S. Open holds a special place in his heart: "That shot at seventeen meant more to me than any golf shot I ever made."

FINAL STANDINGS—TOP PLAYERS

Rank	Player	R1	R2	R3	R4	Total	Par	Money
1	Tom Watson	72	72	68	70	282	-6	$60,000
2	Jack Nicklaus	74	70	71	69	284	-4	$34,506
3T	Bill Rogers	70	73	69	74	286	-2	$14,967
3T	Dan Pohl	72	74	70	70	286	-2	$14,967
3T	Bobby Clampett	71	73	72	70	286	-2	$14,967
6T	David Graham	73	72	69	73	287	-1	$8,011
6T	Lanny Wadkins	73	76	67	71	287	-1	$8,011
6T	Jay Haas	75	74	70	68	287	-1	$8,011
6T	Gary Koch	78	73	69	67	287	-1	$8,011
10T	Bruce Devlin	70	69	75	74	288	Even	$6,332
10T	Calvin Peete	71	72	72	73	288	Even	$6,332

Watson hugs his caddie after his victory. He beat four-time Open winner Nicklaus with birdies on the last two holes.

Tom Watson holds up the U.S. Open Golf Championship trophy following his win at Pebble Beach, California, on June 20, 1982. Watson defeated Jack Nicklaus by two strokes and finished at six under par.

27

The Rally Off Rivera

November 4, 2001, Bank One Ballpark, Phoenix, Arizona

It wasn't just the seventh game of the 2001 World Series that featured a dramatic come-from-behind finish. It was the whole Series. At least that's the way it seemed. In fact, there truly were three come-from-behind ninth-inning dramas, all packed into one five-day stretch.

It was a strange Series. No team ever lost a home game, but three games—Games 4, 5, and 7—featured ninth-inning heroics and the usual combination of heroes and goats. The Yankees had won three Series in a row and were seeking a "four-peat." They found themselves in the ninth inning of Game 7 with the lead and with one of the best closers in history on the mound: Mariano Rivera, who had pitched in 37 consecutive postseason games without a loss, saved 23 postseason games in a row, and held a lifetime 0.70 ERA in the postseason. These were numbers that were simply unreal. ESPN's Jayson Stark wrote, "The odds of getting two runs in the ninth inning off Mariano Rivera are right up there with the odds of going to the moon in a used Hyundai." Rivera had already thrown six shutout innings in the 2001 World Series and had just struck out the side in the eighth inning of Game 7. If all the champagne bottles had already been uncorked, no one could blame the clubhouse attendants.

> ## "That was the greatest Game 7 ever, but I wish it turned out differently."
> —New York City Mayor Rudy Giuliani

But the desert had been good to the Diamondbacks. In their previous three home games, they'd scored a total of 28 runs and yielded only three. Now, headed into the bottom of the ninth inning, they needed a little magic against Rivera as they trailed 2–1 with three outs to go.

Mark Grace, who already had two hits, singled to start off the inning for the D-backs. Damian Miller tried to bunt over pinch runner David Dellucci, but he bunted right back to Rivera; yet, Rivera threw wildly to second and both runners were safe. Pinch hitter Jay Bell tried to bunt, too, but he also blew it, and this time Rivera's throw cut down the lead runner at third. Tony Womack, however, lined a double down the line in right and tied the game as another pinch runner, Midre Cummings, crossed the plate.

With runners on second and third and just one out, Rivera hit Craig Counsell to load the bases. Diamondbacks slugger Luis Gonzalez, who had 57 home runs during the season and 142 RBIs, was up with the winning run 90 feet from home plate. All it took was a little looper over the drawn-in infield to bring Bell in from third and send the delirious crowd home with what the *Boston Globe* headlined as "Desert Reign" delight.

The amazing finish perfectly capped what many observers feel ranks among the greatest World Series ever. With the Yankees one out away from going down three games to one in the Series, veteran Tino Martinez hit the first pitch he saw from 22-year-old Byung-Hyun Kim into the center-field bleachers to tie Game 4 with a two-run, ninth-inning homer.

The game went into extra innings and, in this first Series to stretch into November, Derek Jeter homered to win it. It was the first walk-off homer Jeter had ever had, surprising for the shortstop who seemed to make a career of clutch situations. It was the first time in World Series history that a game-tying homer in the ninth was followed with a game-winning homer in the tenth. Game 5 was almost a rerun of Game 4. Once again, Yankees came from behind in the bottom of the ninth to tie it, and once again they won it in extra innings, though this time it took them 12. Scott Brosius teed off on Arizona's ace reliever, Kim, again to tie the game in the bottom of the ninth, and Alfonso Soriano drove in the game winner in the twelfth. Arizona won a lopsided Game 6 15–2 to tie the Series and set the stage for the Game 7 dramatics in Phoenix.

New York Yankees reliever Mariano Rivera (above) throws against the Arizona Diamondbacks during the eighth inning of Game 7 of the 2001 World Series at Bank One Ballpark in Phoenix.

The Arizona Diamondbacks' Jay Bell (near right) comes home with the winning run on a hit by Luis Gonzalez during the ninth inning.

Gonzalez (far right) raises a fist as he is hugged by coach Eddie Rodriguez.

Maybe Yogi said it best: "Good pitching will beat good hitting anytime!" The fact that he then hedged his bets by adding "and vice versa" is irrelevant here. Arizona GM Joe Garagiola Jr., whose dad was a lifelong pal of Yogi's, obviously agrees. Garagiola loaded up his Diamondbacks with two big guys, Curt Schilling and Randy Johnson, who together carried enough pitching venom to snakebite any hitter in the National League. Between them, they dominated a World Series like no other pair had ever dominated before. To win the two rounds of playoffs—the Division Series and the League Championship Series—and the World Series itself requires eleven postseason victories. Johnson and Schilling won nine of those eleven contests.

In the Division Series, Schilling had won Games 1 and 5 of the best-of-five matchup with the Cardinals. Randy Johnson had lost the second game. In the LCS, it was the "Big Unit"—Randy Johnson—who won Games 1 and 5, while Schilling won Game 3. The D-backs took this set from the Braves, four games to one.

In the World Series itself, Schilling won Game 1, and Johnson won Game 2, Game 6, and Game 7 (in relief of Schilling, who had let up only a single run through seven innings but was pulled for a pinch-hitter).

In the Series, the duo struck out 45 Yankees in $38^2/_3$ innings—and walked only 5. Schilling had a 1.69 Series ERA and Johnson a miserly 1.04. This was the same tag team that had struck out 665 opponents during the regular season, winning 43 games and losing 12.

This was the Series of The Goat That Wasn't, poor Byung-Hyun Kim. A young player, he was far away from home in a strange country. He was also bearing to some degree his nation's hopes and expectations on his shoulders as the first Korean in a World Series. Kim had looked forlorn, about to cry, when he twice failed to get the final out—on back-to-back nights on spirit-crushing home runs.

Had it not been for Randy Johnson and Curt Schilling, Kim may have suffered for months, even years. No wonder the two starters were named co-MVPs for the Series.

Kim, by the way, came back in 2002 and went 8–3 on the year, with a spectacular 2.04 earned run average in a full 98 innings of relief work.

28

And the Band Played On

November 20, 1982, Memorial Stadium, Berkeley, California

John Elway enjoys remembering many games from his college football career at Stanford. There is one game, however, that he would love to forget.

It was the game that forever has been linked to college football history because of "the Play," when California scored the winning touchdown on a five-lateral kickoff return that ended with the Stanford band already on the field.

The 85th game in the history of the Stanford versus California rivalry, played at Memorial Stadium in Berkeley, marked the final game of Elway's college career, and even before he knew how historic the game was going to be, he was upset by the outcome. "What a farce," Elway said. "This was an insult to college football. There's no way it should have happened. They [the officials] ruined my last college football game. It's unbelievable."

Elway's anger came out after Stanford had seemingly won the game on a 35-yard field goal by Mark Harmon. The kick gave the Cardinals a 20–19 lead, and only four seconds remained on the clock.

All Stanford had to do was prevent a miracle kickoff return for a touchdown to complete the victory. Harmon kicked a squib kick, and Cal's Kevin Moen picked up the ball at his own 43. As he started to run, he was about to be tackled when he lateraled the ball to Richard Rodgers. The

> "As far as I was concerned they were all Stanford players, and I just busted through. The trombone player was just in the wrong place at the wrong time."
>
> —Cal safety Kevin Moen

play still seemed innocent enough, until Rodgers lateraled the ball to Dwight Garner.

As Garner was about to be tackled, he lateraled again to Rodgers. Rodgers in turn lateraled to Mariet Ford, who took off toward the end zone.

At about the same time, the 144-member Stanford band—thinking the ball carrier had been tackled—started to

march onto the field to play its postgame victory song. Instead, the play was still alive, and Ford was running straight toward the band.

When he was about to go down at the 25-yard line, he lateraled the ball to Moen, who had started all of this when he recovered the kick. Moen caught the ball and dodged a tuba player before he ran over a trombone player as he reached the end zone.

The officials huddled for five minutes before declaring the run stood and the touchdown counted, and California had won the game. Their judgment was that none of the California players had done anything illegal and that none of the players were down before they lateraled the ball. The band and fans who were on the field were from Stanford, so any penalty for that would have been against Stanford.

The only argument Stanford could make that might have worked was that one of the laterals was actually an illegal forward pass, but the officials ruled otherwise.

A CENTURY-OLD RIVALRY

The rivalry between Stanford and California is the oldest in West Coast football history, going back to 1892. Games between these two are always exciting. In fact, of the 104 games played, 49 were determined by a touchdown or less.

The 1982 game that ended with a run through the Stanford band was one of five games in the storied California-Stanford Big Game series that were decided on the game's final play.

AMONG THE OTHER GAMES:

1972—A touchdown pass from Vince Ferragamo to Steve Sweeney on the final play of the game lifted California to a 24–21 victory.

1974—Stanford's Mike Langford kicked a 50-yard field goal to give the Cardinals a 22–20 win.

1982—This is the one that required a little help from the band before California won, 25–20.

1990—Kicker John Hopkins nailed a 37-yard field goal to give the Cardinals a 27–25 victory.

2000—In the first overtime game between the two rivals, Stanford emerged a 36–30 victor.

When the Stanford band sashayed onto the field with seconds left in the 1982 Cal-Stanford game, they were mistakenly confident that their team was victorious. Cal's Kevin Moen had something else in mind. Moen, with seconds left, scored the winning touchdown.

Hogan's Triumphant Return

June 8–11, 1950, Merion Golf Club, Ardmore, Pennsylvania

Imagine living in constant pain, a dull ache that sometimes flares into excruciating spasms that almost bring you to your knees. Standing for extended periods of time only aggravates it, to the point that you're forced to grip someone's shoulder for support. But you can't sit down, not even for a moment, so you grit your teeth, steady yourself, and try to focus on your backswing. For this is the 1950 U.S. Open, and you are Ben Hogan, competing for your second U.S. Open title 16 months after nearly dying in a devastating car accident.

In February of 1949, the Texas-born Hogan was coming off a 1948 winning streak of six consecutive victories, including wins in both The Masters and the PGA Championship. And although 1949 had just begun, he had already won two out of four tournaments and finished second to Jimmy Demaret in another. Sadly, Hogan's great good fortune came to an abrupt end on a stretch of Highway 80 between Fort Worth and Van Horn, Texas. On February 2, Hogan's car collided with an oncoming Greyhound bus in a thick fog. Reacting quickly, Hogan threw himself across his wife, Valerie, in the passenger seat to protect her. As a result, she emerged from the wreckage with only minor injuries. Hogan, however, lay pinned in their totaled car for 90 minutes until the ambulance arrived.

> **"As you walk down the fairway of life you must smell the roses, for you only get to play one round."**
> —Ben Hogan

Two hours later, doctors at an El Paso hospital admitted Hogan to the emergency room with a broken pelvis, shoulder, ankle, and rib. As if these injuries weren't severe enough, the impact of the collision had mangled his legs. Surgery and a lengthy convalescence followed, but given the extent of his injuries, few thought Hogan would ever play golf professionally again. Yet by the end of the year, Hogan was back at the course, driving balls at Fort Worth's Colonial Country Club.

Despite chronic pain, Hogan was determined to return to the PGA Tour. Famously stoic, he endured swollen and cramped legs to enter the 1950 Los Angeles Open. Although his opening-round score of 73 was disappointing, he subsequently rebounded and made it into a playoff against Sam Snead, who won by 4 strokes. Hogan's surprisingly strong finish impressed everyone but the golfer himself, who reportedly said, "I still have a long way to go."

The road to the U.S. Open was a difficult one. Competing now left him physically and emotionally drained. His legendary stamina appeared to have deserted him, along with his long backswing.

On Thursday, June 8, the first day of the U.S. Open at the famous Merion Golf Club outside Philadelphia, Hogan got out of bed early to soak in a hot bath, apply liniments, and wrap his legs in elastic bandages to prevent swelling. Competing against a field that included Lloyd Mangrum, Jim Ferrier, Dutch Harrison, and reigning champion Cary Middlecoff, Hogan got off to a slow start in the first round, shooting a 2-over-par 72. With this score, he trailed first-round leader Lee Mackey by 8 strokes.

On Friday, Hogan began playing more like his old self. As thousands of spectators thronged the sidelines, he started moving up in the tournament standings. Then, on the eleventh green, intense pain shot through his legs. Before his legs buckled, Hogan reached to his caddie for support. Somehow he managed to complete the round with a score of 69—just 2 strokes behind Harrison, who had taken over the lead.

Back in his room at Philadelphia's Barclay Hotel, Hogan soaked in a tub filled with hot water and Epsom salts. Saturday's back-to-back rounds promised to be particularly brutal. Exhausted from the pain and sleeplessness, he steeled himself for the next day's endurance test.

By sheer force of will, Hogan made it through the third round, but just barely. At the thirteenth hole, his legs cramped so painfully that he nearly quit right then and there. Instead, he staggered through the rest of the round to finish with a respectable 72. He was now 2 strokes behind Mangrum, who topped the standings with a score of 211, 1 over par.

Mangrum's lead evaporated in the fourth round, which saw Hogan take the lead after the first nine holes. Ignoring the pain, he continued to widen his lead by 3 strokes, but the strain was clearly wearing on him. As the throbbing in his legs intensified, Hogan's game began to fall apart. His lead gone, Hogan nervously approached the 448-yard, par-4 eighteenth hole. Unless he made par, which would put him in a playoff against Mangrum and George Fazio, Hogan would be out of contention.

After hitting a solid driver, Hogan limped to the ball for his second shot. If he didn't nail this one, it would be all over.

Using a 1 iron, Hogan swung. The ball sailed toward the green and landed 40 feet from the hole. The crowd burst into wild applause. Hogan 2-putted for a spot in the 18-hole playoff against Mangrum and Fazio. The next day, Hogan prevailed in the playoff, defeating Mangrum and Fazio with a score of 69 to their scores of 73 and 75, respectively. The golfer nicknamed Bantam Ben was back.

Ben Hogan blasts from the sand trap on the twelfth hole during the third round of the U.S. Open Golf Championship at Ardmore, Pennsylvania, on June 11, 1950. He wound up with a 37-35-72 for a third-round total of 213 and an early three-way tie for third.

Hogan holds his trophy. The presenter of the trophy (at right) is James D. Standish Jr., president of the United States Golf Association. Standing at left is Hogan's wife, Valerie. Hogan defeated Lloyd Mangrum and George Fazio in a playoff following a three-way tie.

30

Montana's Super Drive

January 22, 1989, Joe Robbie Stadium, Miami

For most of the San Francisco 49ers fans at Super Bowl XXII in Miami, a field goal at the end of regulation was all they wanted. After all, the three points would tie the game at 16 and send it into overtime.

For a while, that's what quarterback Joe Montana was thinking as well.

"We just got going, thinking field goal," Montana said. "We never gave up. Things might go wrong, but you've got to fight back. That's one thing we never gave up on—confidence. And it showed."

It also helped the 49ers that they had Montana running their offense. Even though he had not done anything spectacular so far in the game and the Bengals were leading, 16–13, Montana and his faithful knew his history of engineering late-game comebacks.

Even when the possession started at the 49ers 8-yard line with just over three minutes to play, he didn't panic, calling two plays at a time and methodically moving his team down the field toward the potential tying field goal. He didn't go

for the dramatic big play, but instead was content to pick away with short and medium passes.

Before the Bengals knew what was happening, Montana had the 49ers at the Cincinnati 35. When he saw Jerry Rice going opposite a man-to-man defense, he

> ## "I don't know of anybody who can play as well in the clutch as Joe does."
> —Bengals coach Sam Wyche

thought touchdown, but he overthrew his star receiver for his only incomplete pass of the drive.

"I was sitting there screaming as loud as I could [at himself] and I hyperventilated," Montana said. "I got dizzy. I almost called timeout, but it faded away."

Unfortunately for the Bengals, Montana recovered quickly. Even a 10-yard penalty on guard Randy Cross on the next play only proved to be a temporary reprieve for Cincinnati. It brought up a second-and-20 on the Cincinnati 45, and once

more the thought of just going for the tying field goal flashed through Montana's mind.

He found Rice open with a 13-yard pass, but Rice then picked up another 14 on the run, making it a 27-yard gain. Now at the 18-yard line, Montana went to another of his favorite targets, Roger Craig, to pick up another eight yards.

The 49ers were now at the Bengals 10, an almost gimme field goal, but Montana now decided to get greedy—why settle for the tie when you had a chance to go for the win and avoid the uncertainty of the sudden-death period?

He called a pass play designed to go to Craig, but he was covered by the Cincinnati defense. Montana searched the field and found the secondary receiver, John Taylor, for the touchdown with 34 seconds to play, giving the 49ers a 20–16 victory. It was Taylor's first reception of the game.

Counting the 10 yards for the penalty, Montana had moved the 49ers 102 yards, completing eight of nine passes for 97 yards.

"Taylor was lined up at the tight end," said Bengals safety Ray Horton. "It didn't pose a problem until Rice came in motion to that side. When he came I had to widen out a little bit, widen my area of responsibility. It gave Taylor more room to operate. He shot right inside. Before I could react, the ball was in there."

For the game, Montana completed 23 of 36 passes for a Super Bowl–record 357 yards. Eleven of his passes went to Rice, who scored the 49ers' first touchdown and set another record with 215 receiving yards.

In Montana's third Super Bowl, he extended his total to 93 passes thrown without an interception, as the 49ers won their third NFL championship.

And he once again earned universal praise for engineering the game-winning drive.

"We had them on their 8 with three minutes to go," said Cincinnati receiver Cris Collinsworth. "Somebody came up to me and said, 'We got them now.' I said, 'Have you taken a look at who's quarterbacking the San Francisco 49ers?' That's what it comes down to. Joe Montana is not human."

MONTANA'S SUPER BOWL COMEBACK

San Francisco's fourth-quarter comeback marked the fifth time in Super Bowl history that a team had rallied to win when they were losing at the end of the third quarter.

Super Bowl V, 1971—Baltimore trailed Dallas, 13–6, but rallied to win, 16–13

Super Bowl X, 1976—Pittsburgh trailed Dallas, 10–7, before rallying to win, 21–17

Super Bowl XIV, 1980—Pittsburgh trailed Los Angeles, 19–17, but came back to win, 31–19

Super Bowl XVII, 1983—Washington trailed Miami, 17–13, but came back to win, 27–17

Super Bowl XXIII, 1989—San Francisco trailed Cincinnati, 13–6, before rallying behind Montana to win, 20–16.

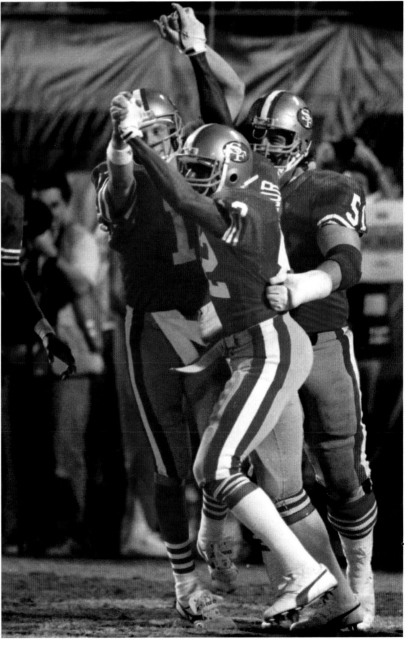

San Francisco 49ers wide receiver Jerry Rice (No. 80, above) dives into the end zone for a touchdown during third-quarter action in Super Bowl XXIII. The touchdown tied the score at 13–13.

San Francisco 49ers quarterback Joe Montana (No. 16, at right) and wide receiver John Taylor (No. 82) clasp hands after Montana's pass to Taylor at the end of the fourth quarter resulted in a 20–16 victory.

Honorable Mention

31

Henderson Stuns Halos

October 12, 1986, Anaheim Stadium, Anaheim, California

On October 12, 1986, the Red Sox faced the Angels in what was potentially the Sox's last game of the postseason. "We were one pitch away from a long winter," reflected Boston's Don Baylor in the middle of a jubilant Red Sox locker room after the game. Boston had just come from behind to win Game 5 of the 1986 American League Championship Series, narrowly escaping elimination. "We lost the night before after leading," said Baylor, "and we were about to lose this game after leading, too. A lot of guys would have taken a lot of bitterness home with them."

Baylor had figured in Boston's comeback and ultimate eleventh-inning victory, but it was Dave Henderson who took the blame for the near defeat and the credit for the win.

The Sox took a 2–0 lead in the second on Rich Gedman's homer off Mike Witt, and were up 2–1 when Henderson lost an Angels fly ball in the sun; it dropped for a double. On the very next play, Henderson snared a Bobby Grich deep fly ball—only

to have it pop out of his glove and over the fence as his wrist hit the barrier. It was a "tip-in" home run, and the Angels took a 3–2 lead, padding it to 5–2 a couple of innings later.

Baylor then blasted a two-run homer in the top of the ninth, closing the gap to 5–4. With two outs and no one on,

> "There were sixty-four thousand people all in their starting blocks waiting to get out on the field. Basically I was looking for a way to get back to our dugout after I struck out."
>
> —Red Sox outfielder Dave Henderson

Gedman came to the plate. He already had managed three hits off Witt, prompting Angels manager Gene Mauch to bring in reliever Gary Lucas. Lucas' first offering hit Gedman, bringing Henderson to the plate. Already wearing the goat's horns, Henderson appeared

destined to make the final out of Boston's year. Mauch brought in Donnie Moore to seal the series for the Angels. Henderson worked the count to 2–2. The Angels were just one strike away from the pennant.

Boston manager John McNamara later recalled, "I saw [Angel designated hitter] Reggie [Jackson] take his cap and sunglasses off. . . . They were collecting the caps so they wouldn't be stolen by the crowd."

After fouling off two more pitches, Henderson drove a stunning home run into the left-field seats for a 6–5 lead. The Angels got another run in the ninth, pushing the game into extra innings, but Henderson's eleventh-inning sacrifice fly off of Moore won it for the Sox, 7–6.

Moore was despondent, a depression that took deeper root as the Angels were eliminated when Boston won both Game 6 and Game 7 back in Boston. Henderson would feature in an equally turbulent game less than two weeks later, a game that left Bill Buckner with even bigger goat horns than Moore's. But for now, it was the Boston Red Sox's turn to shine.

Boston's Dave Henderson (above left) and Rich Gedman celebrate after Henderson's ninth-inning homer gave the Sox a one-run lead.

FALLEN ANGEL

By all rights, the Angels should have won the 1986 ALCS.

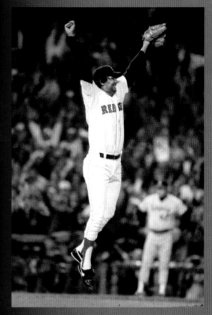

They breezed into the bottom of the ninth inning, at home, with a 5–2 lead. Bill Deane has calculated that they had at least a 97.7 percent probability of winning Game 5 and therefore a 99.4 percent chance of winning that Series.

Well, guess what? Dave Henderson and the Red Sox exploited that miniscule 2.3 percent gap and won the game.

Angels reliever Donnie Moore felt badly. Who wouldn't? So badly that he would commit suicide? That would seem a little extreme. Yet Donnie Moore did take his own life less than three years later, and his agent, Dave Pinter, said with sadness, "Ever since Henderson's home run, he was extremely depressed. He couldn't get over it. He blamed himself for the Angels not going to the Series."

So did a lot of Angels fans. Still, a lot of teams don't make it to the World Series. It happens every year, and, as this book of dramatic come-from-behind finishes in sport demonstrates, there's often one individual who seems to be at each focal point of the drama—the hero and the goat.

Moore certainly had other problems at the time of his suicide. He and his wife had separated just a month before. His career as a ballplayer was just about over; he'd been cut by a minor league team. His finances were in a shambles. His depression from this one playoff game may have contributed to those disappointments as well.

There were a number of reasons he didn't perform up to snuff, but in the end, they didn't matter. He threw one unfortunate pitch and Dave Henderson had one fortunate hit.

Angels fans never forgave Moore, though. In his book *Scapegoats*, Christopher Bell wrote, "Fans support a team with their hearts, and when their hearts are unexpectedly broken they lash out at the player like a scorned lover." Moore's fans were not so angelic; they turned on him and rode him for the next couple of years with derisive catcalls and signs.

They must have forgotten that even after the Henderson homer, the Angels team still had to lose two more games in a row before the Red Sox could advance to the World Series. Two defensive errors let in seven unearned Red Sox runs in Game 7. It wasn't Donnie Moore's fault that his teammates lost both games.

If anyone should have been upset, it should have been manager Gene Mauch. He'd managed the Phillies back in 1964 when the team blew a six-and-a-half-game lead in the month of September. Ahead two games to none in the best-of-five 1982 ALCS, his Angels managed to lose three straight—and that year's pennant. They were just three games behind in 1984, and just one game behind in 1985.

Mauch never made it to a Series.

32

Notre Dame Stops the Streak

January 19, 1974, Notre Dame Athletic and Convention Center, South Bend, Indiana

With just more than three minutes to play, it looked almost certain that UCLA was going to beat Notre Dame and extend their record winning streak to 89 games.

The Bruins led the Fighting Irish by 11 points, 70–59, with 3:22 to play in South Bend after twice leading by as many as 17 points in the first half. UCLA center Bill Walton was back in the lineup after missing three games because of a back injury, and it didn't appear that Notre Dame had enough weapons to wipe out that UCLA lead.

Irish coach Digger Phelps and his team, however, were not in a quitting mood.

Phelps called timeout and inserted freshman Ray Martin into the lineup in place of Bill Paterno and ordered his team to begin pressing the Bruins.

John Shumate began the rally with a hook shot over Walton, then stole the inbounds pass and scored again. UCLA did get the next pass in bounds, but Adrian Dantley stole the ball at midcourt

and went in for a layup. All of a sudden the score was 70–65.

On their next possession, UCLA, perhaps starting to panic, was called for traveling, turning the ball back over to the Irish. Notre Dame worked the ball to

> ## "That game is one of the biggest moments in my basketball career. I see a highlight of it every year, and I never get tired of seeing it."
> —former Notre Dame forward Adrian Dantley

Gary Brokaw, who made the shot to cut the lead to three points.

It appeared UCLA had finally stopped the Notre Dame surge when Dave Meyers scored on a layup, but he too was called for traveling, which negated the basket.

Brokaw hit a short jumper, and the Irish had cut the lead to one point.

Keith Wilkes took the ball inside for UCLA, but as he went up for a shot he was called for charging—the fifth Bruins

turnover in the last three minutes. There were 45 seconds remaining, and Notre Dame called a play designed for the ball to go to Shumate. When he was covered, however, the pass went to Dwight Clay in the right corner, and he hit the fadeaway jumper with 29 seconds to play, putting Notre Dame ahead 71–70 and sending the crowd into a roaring frenzy.

The Bruins still had plenty of time and called timeout with 21 seconds left to set up a play for the winning shot. Tommy Curtis missed a 25-foot shot, Meyers missed the tip-in, and as Walton was grabbing for the ball with six seconds left, a Notre Dame player knocked it out of bounds. The inbounds pass went to Walton, but he missed a 12-foot shot, and two tip-in chances failed as time ran out. Notre Dame had defeated the Bruins and snapped the record winning streak.

Said Phelps, whose team had been second to UCLA in the national polls: "I'm sure everyone was rooting for us the way they used to root against the Yankees. The kids never gave up and were incredible, just unbelievable."

A STREAK OF 88 WINS

Before the UCLA winning streak was snapped at 88 games by Notre Dame, the Bruins survived some close calls to keep the streak alive. The closest call was a 65–64 win over Maryland on December 1, 1973, in the second game of the season.

Another close call came early in the streak. On February 12, 1971, UCLA won 67–65 at Corvallis against Oregon State. During the streak, Corvallis proved a tough place for UCLA to play, even though the Bruins always won. In 1972, UCLA won 78–72, and in 1974 they won 61–57. Oregon State finally broke through and beat UCLA, 78–67, in 1980.

UCLA was also known for winning when the games really counted. During the Bruins' "wonder years," they had another streak going—tournament wins. They won nine national championships from 1964 through 1973 before losing to North Carolina State in the 1974 Final Four. It took a double overtime to give the Wolfpack an 80–77 victory.

Former Bruin Bill Walton said he doesn't expect to see another basketball dynasty like that UCLA run. "The dream of being part of a great college basketball team is not there," he explained. "Unless things turn around in our culture, it's not going to happen anytime soon."

The spoilers (above left): Notre Dame's squad stopped the UCLA juggernaut in a tight 1974 battle that proved to be one of the most exciting NCAA basketball games of all time.

Notre Dame's Gary Brokaw hit a short jumper to cut UCLA's lead to one point. It would be Brokaw's teammate, Dwight Clay, who got the glory shot seconds later.

33

Smart's Swish

March 30, 1987, Louisiana Superdome, New Orleans

The NCAA basketball tournament is called March Madness for a reason. A great season of basketball is whittled down to four teams—and then two—vying for the right to be called champions. But are they really the most talented team or just the luckiest? Games are often won by a single point. Three-pointers, free throws, turnovers, or a lack of timeouts can make or break a team in the waning seconds of a game. And coaching savvy is certainly a plus, as well. It's crazy.

At the end of March 1987, a field of 64 teams had dwindled to 2. Indiana and Syracuse were left to face each other at the Superdome in New Orleans.

Syracuse's starting lineup consisted of two solid seniors, Greg Monroe and Howard Triche, along with junior Rony Seikaly, sophomore Sherman Douglas, and freshman Derrick Coleman.

The Indiana Hoosiers brought a similar group to the court. Seniors Steve Alford and Daryl Thomas were experienced players. They were joined by sophomore Ricky Calloway and two junior

college transfers, Dean Garrett and Keith Smart. The lead went back and forth during the first half, ending with Indiana leading, 34–33, as the teams went into the locker room.

The Orangemen took over after halftime, controlling the scoreboard through most of the half. At one point, Syracuse

> "I wasn't surprised I got the ball—I was surprised it went in."
> —Indiana guard Keith Smart

led by as many as eight points. But along came Indiana's 6'1" junior guard Smart.

Coach Bobby Knight had benched Smart earlier in the game for a bad pass. Words were exchanged, with the implication that Smart needed to produce fast or he would be spending the rest of the game on the sidelines.

Syracuse had a five-point lead with 7:22 left on the clock when Smart went back in. He took his coach's challenge to heart, making layups and bank shots with

a golden touch and scoring 13 points in the second half. But, although Smart scored 12 of the Hoosiers' final 15 points, the Orangemen were still wary of Alford, who had a game-high 23 points.

In front of 64,959 fans at the Superdome, Syracuse found themselves leading, 73–72, with 28 seconds to go. Coleman drew a foul and went to the line for a one-and-one chance for the Orangemen. Knight called a timeout before Coleman took his shots, and suddenly Indiana knew they would have a chance to at least tie the game. Knight drew up a play, hoping to get the ball into the hands of Alford, the Hoosiers' most reliable shooter. But basketball is a game, and plays don't always turn out as planned.

Coleman was not able to benefit from his trip to the charity stripe. He missed and the rebound went to Smart. Aware of Alford's steady hand, Syracuse was covering the senior, and Smart passed off to Thomas. He too was covered and passed the ball back to Smart. With five seconds remaining, Smart sunk a 16-footer from the corner of the baseline.

Syracuse got the ball back with only seconds on the clock. A long pass downcourt was intercepted by Smart, and Indiana won it, 74–73.

If his two previous championship teams had been "destined to win," what did Knight have to say about his 1987 Hoosiers? "This team went way beyond what I thought its potential was," he said. "They were unwilling to lose."

Syracuse's Howard Triche (No. 25) tries to stop Indiana's Keith Smart from making a shot in the final moments of the 1987 NCAA championship game at the Superdome in New Orleans. The basket put Indiana ahead 74–73, ultimately giving them the victory.

34

Affirmed's Triple Crown

June 10, 1978, Belmont Park, Elmont, New York

In horse racing, there have been numerous rivalries over the years, but none as great or as poignant as the one between thoroughbreds Affirmed and Alydar. When Seattle Slew won the Triple Crown in 1977, racing enthusiasts were prepared to wait years to crown another winner, but throughout the 1978 season Alydar and Affirmed battled to win each of the big races. Could one of them pull out a Triple Crown victory? Or would the other horse be the spoiler?

In many ways, these horses were more alike than they were different. Both were chestnut colts born in 1975, Alydar at the renowned Calumet Farm in Kentucky and Affirmed at Harbor View Farm in Florida. Harbor View owners Louis and Patrice Wolfson had entered previous horses in the Kentucky Derby, but without great success.

Affirmed began his career on May 24, 1977, at Belmont Park, winning the race by four and a half lengths. Three weeks later Affirmed and Alydar met for the first time at the Youthful Stakes. Affirmed won that race, taking the lead in the stretch and holding on to win by a neck. It was Alydar's first race, and he came in a distant fifth.

It was the start of an unparalleled competition between the two-year-olds.

> "He was just a horse of tremendous courage. He loved to race. He was a great horse to ride."
>
> —jockey Steve Cauthen

The pair met up again at the Great American Stakes, where Alydar won by three and a half lengths, handing Affirmed his first defeat.

The colts separated for the winter, with Alydar heading to Florida and Affirmed training in California. Both dominated races in their respective areas before the rivalry was once again ignited in the spring of 1978 at Churchill Downs, home of the Kentucky Derby.

The three-year-old chestnuts were both strong, beautiful, and proven winners. The Calumet Farm reputation of eight previous Derby wins gave Alydar the slight edge. He was the 6-to-5 favorite, with Affirmed at 9-to-5. Affirmed had never been beaten by a horse other than Alydar, and thoroughbred fans watched with anticipation as the pair prepared to race for the roses.

Third-rated Sensitive Prince turned on the early speed, leading the pack entering the first turn. Raymond Earl was in second place, and jockey Steve Cauthen, riding Affirmed, seemed content to let his mount linger in third. Believe It made a short-lived claim on the lead before Affirmed moved past him in the stretch. Alydar made his own powerful move past Believe It, but it wasn't enough to catch Affirmed, who won the first leg of the Triple Crown by one and a half lengths.

Two weeks later the pair traveled to Pimlico, Maryland, for the site of yet another face-off. This time it was the Preakness Stakes.

"When these horses got together, it was electrifying," John Veitch, Alydar's trainer, said. "You knew you were going to see a horse race, and you knew that at any time one could beat the other. And you always knew they were going to put on a show for you."

From the start the Preakness was a closer race than the Derby had been. Affirmed had an early lead, but jockey Jorge Velasquez, who had been criticized for waiting too long before making a move in the Derby, spurred Alydar into action. In one of the most famous races in Preakness history, Alydar slowly gained on his rival throughout the backstretch. The two were side by side leaving the turn and battled all the way down the stretch before Affirmed fought off his challenger and won by a neck.

Only three weeks after the Preakness, the rivals met in New York to compete for the final jewel of the Triple Crown—the Belmont Stakes. In front of a crowd of 65,417 frenzied fans, the horses prepared to run the race of their lives. Horse handicappers thought this might just be the race that belonged to Alydar. The 12-furlong length was the longest of the three races, enough for him to make his break and keep it.

There was a five-horse field, but to Affirmed and Alydar, there was only one horse to beat. After a half mile, the pair was first and second, with Affirmed leading by a mere length. By midrace, they were running neck and neck. Adding to the excitement, Alydar took a slight lead coming down the stretch, but Affirmed dug into his own reserve and gave it one last push. At the wire, it was Affirmed by a head.

The chestnut colt from Harbor View Farm won the 1978 Belmont Stakes and the Triple Crown. But two horses of that year will go down in history as proud competitors, rivals, and champions.

Steve Cauthen (above) celebrates while riding Affirmed.

Affirmed, on the inside, wins the Belmont Stakes and the Triple Crown ahead of Alydar in Elmont, New York, June 10, 1978.

35

Carter Crushes Philly

October 23, 1993, SkyDome, Toronto

It's a fact of life in the Great White North: most Canadian sports heroes are missing at least some of their front teeth, wear skates, perform best on ice, and hail from places such as Flin Flon, Medicine Hat, or Moose Jaw.

Joe Carter is the exception that proves the rule. The former Blue Jay star wore cleats instead of blades, flashed a perfect, pearly smile, and hailed from Oklahoma City, Oklahoma. And the only ice associated with the 6'3", 215-pound Carter was the ice water in his veins as he stepped to the plate on Saturday, October 23, 1993, in front of 52,195 fans at Skydome in Toronto.

The question on everybody's mind throughout the roller-coaster 1993 Series was whether the fat lady would be singing "The Star-Spangled Banner" or "Oh Canada." The year before she had sung the Canadian anthem in both official languages, and Canada had gone baseball crazy in the wake of its first World Series championship.

This year the National League champion Philadelphia Phillies were hoping to change her tune and bring the title back to U.S. soil.

The Blue Jays had only been in existence since 1977, and yet they had already set a new baseball attendance record: more fans had come to see the Jays at Skydome than had turned out in New York, Chicago, Los Angeles, or any

> "They haven't made up the word yet to describe the feeling. Once the ball goes over the fence, it's something you can't believe."
>
> —Blue Jays designated hitter Joe Carter

other American baseball mecca. The Phillies, who had finished dead last in 1992, had earned their way into the fall classic by upsetting the heavily favored Atlanta Braves in six games in the National League Championship Series. They were a team of characters: guys like Mitch "Wild Thing" Williams, Len "Nails" Dykstra, and longhaired, tobacco-juice-stained John Kruk. They were the kind of friends you'd like to have behind you in a bar fight but would not invite to your wedding. The defending champion Blue Jays—a much more conservative lot—also needed six games to defeat the Chicago White Sox for American League supremacy.

In Game 1, the Blue Jays, on the strength of homers by Devon White and American League batting champion John Olerud, defeated Curt Schilling and the Phillies, 8–5. Al Leiter, pitching in relief, picked up the win.

With Terry Mulholland on the mound, the Phillies fought back in Game 2, scoring five runs in the third inning on their way to a 6–4 victory to knot the Series. Carter homered for Toronto as starter Dave Stewart absorbed the loss.

The Series returned to Philadelphia for Game 3, which the Jays won, 10–3, on 13 hits. Game 4 was a slugfest, a 15–14 Blue Jays victory in which both teams seemed to hit everything thrown their way. Then Schilling blanked Toronto 2–0 in Game 5 to send the Series back to Toronto for an historic Game 6.

Paul Molitor's triple sparked the Blue Jays to a 3–1 first-inning lead. Molitor hit a home run in the fifth, extending the lead, 5–1. Meanwhile, the Blue Jays' Stewart pitched brilliantly for six innings, allowing only two hits. In the top of the seventh, however, he began to falter. The big right-hander walked shortstop Kevin Stocker and surrendered a single to second baseman Mickey Morandini. Always dangerous Dykstra then went deep for the fourth time in the Series, sending Stewart to the showers and opening the floodgates for a five-run inning.

The score remained 6–5, Phillies, going into the bottom of the ninth. With Williams now on the mound, Rickey Henderson walked on four pitches. White recorded the first out of the inning on a fly ball, and eventual Series MVP Molitor, who was on a quest for his first World Series ring, singled to center field, bringing Carter to the plate with two men on base. He worked the count to 2–2 and then hit the ball over the left-field fence to give the Blue Jays their second World Series title in two years. It was the first time since Bill Mazeroski's home run in 1960 that the World Series had ended with a home run, and only the second time in history.

Before that ball even landed in the bullpen, Carter had entered the sacred—and formerly exclusive—realm of Maurice "the Rocket" Richard, Frank "the Big M" Mahovlich, Bobby "the Golden Jet" Hull, Bobby Orr, Gordie Howe, and—dare we say it—Wayne "the Great One" Gretzky. In the ninth inning of Game 6 of the 1993 World Series, Carter became a Canadian icon—the Nelson Eddy of Canadian baseball. With one dramatic swing of the bat, he defeated the bad guys, and mushed those huskies to victory. It was only the second time a World Series had been decided by a homer.

In truth, there were many heroes in this World Series. Molitor batted .500 and hit two home runs, driving in eight runs. Duane Ward saved two games and won another, posting a 1.93 ERA. Roberto Alomar batted .480 with six RBIs. The Phillies' Dykstra batted .348, hit four homers, and drove in eight runs. But Carter, with his two home runs and eight RBIs, was the man of the hour, the day, and the year.

Toronto Blue Jays batter Joe Carter watches his ninth-inning, game-winning home run as the Jays defeat the Philadelphia Phillies 8–6 to win their second straight World Series, four games to two, on October 23, 1993, at the SkyDome in Toronto.

The SkyDome erupts in fireworks as Carter crosses home plate with the winning run.

36

The Chicken Soup Game

January 1, 1979, Cotton Bowl, Dallas

At halftime of the Cotton Bowl, Notre Dame quarterback Joe Montana was suffering from the flu. He ate hot chicken noodle soup and took a warm shower, hoping to raise his body temperature, which had been chilled by the 17-degree temperature and minus-6-degree windchill.

Still, coach Dan Devine didn't know if Montana would be able to return to the game against Houston. While Montana was trying to recover enough to play, the Cougars scored twice in the third quarter to increase their lead to 34–12.

"They told us Joe was not coming back and we thought it was over," said center Dave Huffman. "But we learned over the last four years that it's never over. We were terrible for three quarters, but the last seven minutes we played football like we know how."

That was when Montana, playing the last game of his college career, returned and made the Cougars and their fans sick.

"We're going to win," Devine kept telling his players on the sideline. Whether he actually believed that or not, however, is another story.

The Notre Dame comeback began when Tony Belden blocked a punt and freshman Steve Cichy recovered and returned it 33 yards for a touchdown. The Fighting Irish added a two-point conversion on a pass from Montana to Vagas Ferguson to cut Houston's lead to 34–20.

After stopping Houston and forcing a punt, Montana, who had completed only

> ## "Once I got back on the field, I didn't consider my health. I looked at the score and I never thought of losing."
> —Joe Montana

6 of 15 passes for 71 yards in the first half, took over following the 28-yard kick. He led the Irish on another scoring drive, this time taking the ball in himself on a 2-yard run, covering the 61 yards in five plays. Another two-point conversion, on a pass from Montana to Kris Haines, cut the lead to 34–28 with just over four minutes remaining.

Another defensive stop was followed by a 27-yard punt, giving Notre Dame

the ball back with a chance to score the tying touchdown, but Montana was hit by Houston linebacker David Hodge at the end of a 16-yard run and fumbled. Houston recovered, and with only 1:50 to play, it looked as if the comeback attempt had failed.

The Cougars failed to run out the clock, however, and with 46 seconds remaining, they dropped back in punt formation. Notre Dame was offside on the play, and that moved the ball to their 29-yard line, bringing up fourth-and-1. Instead of punting again, Houston coach Bill Yeoman decided to try to pick up the first down.

Emmett King was brought down short of the first down, giving Notre Dame the ball back with 28 seconds remaining.

So Montana and Notre Dame took over, operating with no timeouts. Montana picked up 11 yards after scrambling away from the Houston defenders, then hit Haines for a 10-yard gain as he went out of bounds on the 8-yard line with six seconds left. Devine called for a quick pass to one of the wide receivers, then told Montana if that didn't work, to call whatever play he felt most comfortable running.

Montana tried to throw the ball to Haines, but it fell incomplete. With two seconds left, Montana decided to come back with the same play.

"Joe asked me if I could beat my man again," Haines said. "I said yes. He smiled and said, 'Let's do it.' And we did. It couldn't have been a more perfect pass."

The ball was low and looked like it was headed out of bounds in the corner of the end zone, but that was where Haines expected the ball to be. He caught it, and the game was tied.

Maybe a little overexcited and ready to celebrate, the Irish were called for illegal procedure on the first extra-point attempt, forcing junior Joe Unis to kick from 25 yards out to win the game.

"Of all the comebacks I've been associated with in coaching, this had to be the greatest," said Devine.

Notre Dame split end Kris Haines (top) holds the ball high overhead after catching a touchdown pass from quarterback Joe Montana in the closing seconds of the 1979 Cotton Bowl game in Dallas, Texas. This touchdown tied the score.

Eric Herring (above), University of Houston flanker, is grabbed around the neck by Notre Dame safety Jim Browner (No. 33) and another Notre Dame player after Herring took a pass from quarterback Danny Davis during the second quarter. The play was good for 15 yards.

Pete Pallas (left), Notre Dame fullback, holds the ball with both hands as he goes for a two-yard gain during the first quarter. Making the stop is Houston linebacker David Hodge and coming in to help is nose guard Roger Oglesby.

37

Borg's Fifth Straight Wimbledon Title

July 5, 1980, All-England Club, Wimbledon, England

Over the course of his career, John McEnroe took on many of the world's best tennis players and won, propelled to victory by his ferocious volleys, daredevil physicality, and competitive zeal. A brash and volatile player whose tirades and thrown rackets became the stuff of tennis infamy, he first burst onto Wimbledon in 1977 as an 18-year-old amateur. That year, he made it all the way to the semifinals before losing to Jimmy Connors, 6–3, 6–3, 4–6, 6–4. The tables would be turned three years later, when McEnroe would sweep past Connors to the tournament finals for the first time, where he faced the player he considered both his arch rival and one of the greatest players of all time: Björn Borg.

By the 1980 Wimbledon men's final, Borg had won the tournament four consecutive times—the first player to do this since Tony Wilding, from 1910 to 1913. Nothing, not even the second-seeded McEnroe, was going to come between Borg and a record fifth consecutive title.

Whatever their differences, Borg and McEnroe shared one thing in common: both were driven competitors determined to be number one. And nowhere was this more apparent than that first Saturday in

> "You could definitely feel something in the air that day, more so than I've ever felt anywhere else. That's when I knew this was the way tennis should be."
>
> —John McEnroe

July of 1980, when they played one of the most memorable Wimbledon finals in the tournament's history.

The bane of line judges everywhere, McEnroe had already alienated many of the spectators with his antics during his semifinal match against Connors at the 1980 tournament. Yet even his most vocal critics had to concede that he was a gifted, albeit infuriating, player. In the first

set, the 21-year-old lefty from suburban Long Island put his racket where his mouth was. Relying on his ferocious volleys and speed, McEnroe overpowered Borg to win the first set, 6–1.

Caught off guard by McEnroe's aggressive play, Borg struggled to stay alive in the second set. Finally, in the 12th game, Borg broke McEnroe's serve for the first time with a powerful backhand return. His confidence restored, Borg took the second set, 7–5, and the third set, 6–3.

In the fourth set, Borg broke McEnroe's serve to lead five games to four. Not only did McEnroe twice hold off Borg at match point, but he also went on to win six points in a row and ultimately squared the set at 6 all.

The 1980 fourth-set tiebreaker has gone down in the history books as one of the all-time great moments in tennis. Over the course of 22 grueling minutes, the two waged a fierce battle that ultimately produced 34 contested points—a Wimbledon record. Neither player held the advantage for very long. Borg had five match points—four on his serve—but faltered repeatedly against McEnroe, who finally captured the set in an 18–16 victory that pushed the match well past the three-hour mark. The one-hour, six-minute-long fourth set had taken its toll on McEnroe, who was emotionally and physically spent. Summoning his last bit of energy, he met Borg head-on in the fifth set, but the Swede was not to be denied. Hitting 80 percent of his first serves, he dropped only three points in his seven service games on his way to victory, winning the fifth set eight games to McEnroe's six. Nearly four hours after the match began, Borg kissed the Wimbledon trophy for the fifth and final time. The 1980 men's final proved to be the 24-year-old champion's Wimbledon swan song. The following year, McEnroe and Borg again met in the final, but this time, McEnroe defeated Borg to take the first of his three Wimbledon titles.

Clocking in at 233 minutes, the 1980 Wimbledon showdown between Björn Borg and John McEnroe was the longest men's final in the tournament's history—until the 1982 final, when defending champ McEnroe lost to Jimmy Connors in a match that ran an exhausting 256 minutes, still the record. Here are the 10 longest men's finals in Wimbledon history:

1982: Second-seeded Jimmy Connors defeats top-seeded John McEnroe, 3–6, 6–3, 6–7 (2–7), 7–6 (7–5), 6–4 **Time: 256 minutes**

1980: Top-seeded Björn Borg defeats second-seeded John McEnroe, 1–6, 7–5, 6–3, 6–7 (16–18), 8-6 **Time: 233 minutes**

1981: Second-seeded John McEnroe defeats top-seeded Björn Borg, 4–6, 7–6 (7–1), 7–6 (7–4), 6–4 **Time: 202 minutes**

1985: Unseeded Boris Becker defeats eighth-seeded Kevin Curren, 6–3, 6–7 (4–7), 7–6 (7–3), 6–4 **Time: 198 minutes**

1977: Second-seeded Björn Borg defeats top-seeded Jimmy Connors, 3–6, 6–2, 6–1, 5–7, 6–4 **Time: 194 minutes**

2000: Top-seeded Pete Sampras defeats twelfth-seeded Patrick Rafter, 6–7 (10–12), 7–6 (7–5), 6–4, 6–2 **Time: 182 minutes**

2001: Unseeded Goran Ivanisevic defeats third-seeded Patrick Rafter, 6–3, 3–6, 6–3, 2–6, 9–7 **Time: 181 minutes**

1993: Top-seeded Pete Sampras defeats third-seeded Jim Courier, 7–6 (7–3), 7–6 (8–6), 3–6, 6–3 **Time: 178 minutes**

1990: Third-seeded Stefan Edberg defeats second-seeded Boris Becker, 6–2, 6–2, 3–6, 3–6, 6–4 **Time: 178 minutes**

1998: Top-seeded Pete Sampras defeats fourteenth-seeded Goran Ivanisevic, 6–7 (2–7), 7–6 (11–9), 6–4, 3–6, 6–2 **Time: 172 minutes**

John McEnroe (above) flies through the air in a desperate attempt to reach a shot from Björn Borg.

Borg (left) reacts after defeating McEnroe to win his fifth consecutive Wimbledon singles championship on July 5, 1980.

American Dream

38

July 10, 1999, Rose Bowl, Pasadena, California

Never in the history of professional sports had an American crowd turned out in such force to see women play a sport. The 90,185 fans in the Rose Bowl got their money's worth and then some. The 1999 Women's World Cup came to a dramatic end on a penalty kick off the left foot of American midfielder Brandi Chastain, and the roar of the record-setting crowd could be heard all over Pasadena.

While the finals matchup between the heavily favored American team and a skilled and athletic Chinese team didn't offer many fireworks in 120 minutes of regulation soccer, the quality of play was superb from the start. The two most recognizable stars on the field, USA's Mia Hamm and Sun Wen of China, were held in check by two defenses that had combined to allow only five goals throughout all of their World Cup games leading up to the title event.

The American defensive unit of Carla Overbeck, Kate Sobrero, and Joy Fawcett provided most of the intensity; Team USA's keeper, Briana Scurry, was rarely tested. She finished the game with just two saves, while China's Gao Hong was forced to make only four. Each team

> ## "I saw her [Chinese midfielder Liu Ying's] body language when she was walking up to the penalty spot. I thought, 'This is the one.'"
>
> –American goalkeeper Briana Scurry

spent much of the game fighting to possess the ball in the midfield; the United States was able to run their possession-oriented game, but with little offensive success. Although both Hamm and Sun were able to fire off three shots on goal apiece, quality opportunities were extremely hard to come by.

China, however, missed a golden one in the 100th minute of play on a corner kick by midfielder Liu Ying. Chinese back Fan Yunjie connected on a solid header that Scurry did not have a chance to get to. However, American forward Kristine Lilly was in exactly the right place to come to Scurry's aid, kicking the ball away from the mouth of the goal and preventing a sure tally for China.

The Americans also had their chances. In the eighth minute Hamm barely missed connecting with fellow midfielder Michelle Akers on a free kick from 40 yards out. Just four minutes later, Akers put a long shot on goal that was played cleanly by Gao.

The Americans' precision passing, however, prevented the Chinese from establishing their own attack, and for a large part of the game the midfield of the U.S. team, led as always by veteran Julie Foudy, dominated their counterparts. By far the most experienced team in the third Women's World Cup ever, the Americans were cool under pressure for the entire game. The fact that China had beaten the U.S. squad two out of the three times that they had met in the past year did not seem to intimidate American veterans such as Foudy and Lilly, who had played in 180 games for the national team.

It was exactly this experience on which the American women drew as the game came down to penalty kicks. As per regulation, each team sent five players to take penalty shots in the normal one-on-one scenario. Each team's first two shooters connected as the tension mounted, and all eyes were on goalies Scurry and Gao.

Fresh in the minds of the American fans in attendance was the spectacular play of Scurry in the Americans' semifinal game against an offensively potent Brazilian squad. The inconsistent American keeper had shined, making numerous difficult saves to preserve the 2–0 lead that Team USA's offense had obtained.

Expecting another breathtaking performance from Scurry, the rumble of the crowd grew with each shot, and by the third round of shooting, the noise was deafening. Luckily, Scurry needed only her eyes and instincts against Liu and appeared to guess the third Chinese shooter's placement perfectly. The American keeper made a sprawling save to her left on a well-kicked ball. The crowd was on their feet the second the ball was knocked away, and they remained standing as the aim of each subsequent shooter from Team USA was true.

Overbeck, Fawcett, Lilly, and Hamm all connected on their shots to give Chastain the opportunity to win it on the Americans' fifth and final shot. China had not given in, however, as Xie Huilin, Qiu Haiyan, and captain Sun had all connected on their shots.

As the last American shooter, Chastain had the opportunity to give the American crowd reason to go wild. Having been instructed by coach Tony DiCicco to go with her off-foot against the sure-handed Hong, Chastain fired a hard shot to the right of the Chinese goalkeeper. As the ball squeezed between the diving Hong and the right goal post, the crowd did indeed go wild, and American soccer finally showed its true colors.

Brandi Chastain (top) toasts the U.S. victory by taking off her jersey.

American champions Chastain (left), Julie Foudy (center), and Carla Overbeck (right) after receiving their medals.

Merkle's Blunder

September 23, 1908, Polo Grounds, New York

There are many pathways to baseball immortality. Hit over .400; hit safely in 56 consecutive games; strike out 20 batters in nine innings; or win 30 games, just to name a few. But Fred Merkle had a different way.

If not for one game early in his career, Merkle's name would long ago have faded into anonymity. His statistics—he was a lifetime .273 hitter—would certainly never have marked him for lasting fame. He did, however, manage to survive for 16 years in the major leagues, including a 4-year stint with the Chicago Cubs toward the end of his career. The Cubs must have welcomed him with open arms. After all, he had already won the 1908 pennant for them. Trouble is, he was playing for the New York Giants at the time.

On September 23, 1908, the Cubs and Giants, tied for the league lead, met in a crucial game at the Polo Grounds in New York. Just how crucial it was to become, no one could have imagined. Nor could they have imagined that the result would not be decided until October 8, a full week and a half later. Future Hall of Famer Christy Mathewson was on the mound for the Giants, while the Cubs' fortunes were placed in the hands of Jack Pfiester, a southpaw with a well-deserved reputation as a Giant killer.

Other notables in the cast were the Cubs' lyrical double-play combo of shortstop Joe Tinker, second baseman Johnny Evers,

> ## "We were robbed of it [the pennant] and you can't say that Merkle did it."
>
> ### —Giants manager John McGraw

and first sacker Frank Chance. Evers was the acknowledged leader of the Cubs, and this would be abundantly apparent before this game was over.

In the bottom of the ninth, with the score tied, 1–1, and two out, the Giants had runners on first and third. Al Bridwell then hit a waist-high fastball on a line to right-center field. Fans poured from the stands to join in the celebration, and the Giants headed for the dugout to avoid the crush. Unfortunately, Giants first baseman Fred Merkle was one of them. After watching Moose McCormick cross home plate, Merkle, running toward second base, wheeled and trotted from the field, believing the game was over. The Cubs' Evers knew better. He knew that the force play at second would erase the run and take the game to extra innings.

Amid the chaos, Evers stood on second and pleaded for someone to throw him the ball. Umpire Hank O'Day, realizing what was happening, allowed events to unfold. Outfielder Solly Hofman threw the ball in. It was a bizarre scene, with Giants coach Joe McGinnity trying to run interference and prevent the Cubs from seizing the ball—and the day. Two Cubs battled him for the ball, but McGinnity emerged from the scrum and was able to throw it toward the stands, where several New York fans got involved in the strange tableau. Cubs benchwarmer Kid Kroh body checked them out of the way and threw the ball— or at least *a* ball (some claimed it was not the game ball at all)—to third baseman Harry Steinfeldt, who lateraled it to Tinker, who relayed it to Evers. Umpire O'Day then made one of the gutsiest calls in baseball history. He called Merkle out and announced that McCormick's run did not count.

There was bedlam in Gotham. The fans were celebrating the Giants' win, blissfully unaware that the score was still tied. O'Day retreated to the safety of the clubhouse to deliver his verdict. When the fans discovered the truth, a mini riot took place, making further play impossible.

The tie game caused repercussions throughout the league. There were hearings, protests, and counterprotests. After all was said and done, beleaguered National League president Harry Pulliam announced his decision: the game would be replayed in its entirety after the season only if it had a bearing on the final standings. This decision pleased no one, but it stuck.

The pennant race continued to career toward its tumultuous conclusion.

When the final game of the season had gone into the record books, the Cubs and Giants were tied with 98 wins and 55 losses each. A win in the September 23 game would have given either team the pennant.

On October 8, they played that game over. Despite its importance, the contest featured none of the vaudeville-style theatrics of the previous month's debacle. More than forty thousand Giants fans showed up to watch their hero, Mathewson, reap revenge on the Cubs and the hierarchy of baseball. Unfortunately, Mathewson did not pitch like a Hall of Famer on this day. The Cubs won the game, 4–2, capturing the National League pennant and resurrecting criticism of "Bonehead" Fred Merkle.

Umpire Hank O'Day (right) declared the game a 1–1 tie when the Cubs appealed by touching second. Merkle was called out.

Fred Merkle (above, in a photograph taken when he was the coach of the New York Yankees) became baseball's biggest goat when he failed to touch second base on what would have been a game-winning hit by teammate Al Bridwell—a mistake that would cost the Giants the 1908 pennant.

40

Mr. Clutch Delivers

April 29, 1970, the Forum, Inglewood, California

In the late spring of 1970, with a squad consisting of the legendary Willis Reed and Walt Frazier, the New York Knicks seemed in good position to take home their first piece of NBA hardware.

After dispatching Baltimore and Milwaukee in the Eastern Conference playoffs, however, the Knicks found themselves staring up at the West Coast juggernaut Los Angeles Lakers, led by the 7'1" Wilt Chamberlain and "Mr. Clutch" Jerry West.

Chamberlain, however, had not yet fully recovered from knee surgery, and legendary forward Elgin Baylor was clearly beyond his prime. The 31-year-old West was still going strong, but the opinion of most observers was that the cohesive Knicks would have no problem dispatching a slower and less aggressive Los Angeles club.

But after the Knicks ran the Lakers off the Madison Square Garden floor in a 124–112 Game 1 victory, the Lakers responded by following West's 34 points to a 105–103 victory and an even series.

By the time the fourth quarter of Game 3 rolled around, it had become a nip-and-tuck contest, with the teams trading the lead as the game wound down. With just 18 seconds left in regulation and the Knicks trailing 99–98, Dick Barnett connected to put the Knicks up by a

> ## "The man's crazy. He looks determined. He thinks it's really going in."
>
> —Knicks guard Walt Frazier

single point. On the ensuing Lakers possession, Barnett astutely fouled Chamberlain, a notoriously poor free throw shooter. Chamberlain missed the first but canned the second, giving the Knicks an opportunity to win the game with 15 seconds left. This time it would be Dave DeBusschere who would take the shot, a 17-foot jumper that fell through the iron with only three ticks remaining.

The Lakers, ever cool-headed, wasted not one of those ticks. Chamberlain took the inbounds and flicked it down the court to West, who came free of Knicks defenders about 10 feet behind the midcourt line. The man known for his ability to hit the big shot then delivered an overarm, one-handed bomb that traveled nearly 60 feet before finding the bottom of the net. As the Los Angeles crowd screamed, yelled, and danced in the stands, the scoreboard flickered and changed to read the score: 102–102. The game was tied on a shot that, had the three-point line existed in 1970, would have been one of the all-time greatest game-winning shots in NBA history. As it was, however, the game went into overtime, and the Knicks escaped with the win despite West's 34-point, one-prayer performance.

The Knicks would go on to win the classic matchup in seven thrilling games, most notably Game 5, in which they came from behind to win despite the absence of Reed. Although Reed returned to the court for Game 7, it was Game 3 that has lived on as both the turning point of the series and one of the greatest finishes in NBA Finals history.

Jerry West (left) and Elgin Baylor both go up for a rebound against the Knicks in the 1970 NBA Finals.

JERRY WEST, "MR. CLUTCH"

Although Jerry West won only a single NBA championship in his 14 years with the Los Angeles Lakers, he will always be remembered as a player whose best moments came when his team most needed him. While the 60-footer against the Knicks remains his most famous clutch performance, here are a few career highlights of the man whose silhouette graces the NBA logo to this day.

In 1962, West's second year in the NBA, the Lakers met the Celtics in the NBA Finals. At the end of the third game of the series, with the contest in jeopardy, West scored two straight jumpers to tie the game. With three seconds remaining, West then stole Sam Jones' inbounds pass, dribbled to the hoop, and floated in a layup to win the game for Los Angeles.

In 1963, in the Division Finals against St. Louis, West duplicated his incredible feat. With the Lakers having come back from a late seven-point deficit, West once again pounced on an inbounds pass, this one from Cliff Hagan, and nailed a jumper to win the game.

In 1965, West averaged 40.6 points per game during the Lakers' 11-game postseason run. Against the Baltimore Bullets in the Division Finals, West averaged an astonishing 46.3 points per contest.

In 1966, West averaged 34.2 points per game in 14 playoff games for the Lakers as they were eliminated once again by the Boston Celtics in the NBA Finals.

Matched up against the Celtics dynasty in the NBA Finals again in 1969, West watched in frustration as his Lakers failed yet again to win the championship. Despite this, West became the only player ever to be named Finals MVP without being on the winning squad. The award was well deserved. In Game 7, playing with an injured leg, West netted 42 points, 13 rebounds, and 12 assists.

41

The Milan Miracle

March 20, 1954, Hinkle Fieldhouse, Butler University, Indianapolis

It was a classic story of David and Goliath, the kind Hollywood loves. When *Hoosiers* was released in 1986, it touched a responsive chord in millions. The story of dedication, sacrifice, and team-work extolled values that are cherished by sports fans and non–sports fans alike. It also made national celebrities out of Marvin Wood and Bobby Plump, the coach and star player of the real-life team on which the movie was based.

At the time, all high schools in Indiana competed in one statewide tournament, regardless of their size (unlike most other states where schools are grouped into divisions according to enrollment). Even the smallest school—and Milan, with 161 students, certainly was among Indiana's smallest—could dream of going to Indianapolis and being crowned the best basketball team in the state.

Wood preached a patient offense based on passing and teamwork and holding the ball for a good shot. "Woody was a coach ahead of his time, at least in southeastern Indiana," said Plump. "He

brought a disciplined offense to our part of the state, which up to that time had been schooled mainly on freelance basketball."

Wood figured that the best chance for Milan to beat bigger schools was to dictate the tempo of the game and make the opponent play Milan's style and not theirs.

> ## "It was a once-in-a-lifetime deal. We beat supposedly the best in the state. Nobody was supposed to beat Muncie Central."
> —Milan forward Ken Wendelman

That formula helped Milan reach the tournament semifinals in 1953, so its march to the title in 1954 wasn't a total surprise, but it was remarkable nevertheless.

Milan faced a stern test in the Regional Finals when it went up against a bigger and more athletic team, Crispus Attucks of Indianapolis, which featured a sophomore named Oscar Robertson, who would go on to a Hall of Fame career.

Wood thought about going into a total stall but rejected the idea, showing enough confidence in his team to let them play their regular, deliberate style. Milan responded with a 65–52 win to advance to the Final Four, handing Robertson his only defeat in 28 state tournament games.

Milan defeated Terre Haute Gerstmeyer, 60–48, in the semifinals, but Bob Engel, one of Milan's biggest players, suffered a back injury. Wood knew that more than ever he'd have to control the pace in the final against Muncie Central, a much larger school that had won eight state titles and had been to the Final Four 17 times. Muncie's front-court players stood 6'5", 6'4", and 6'2"; Milan's tallest players were Ron Truitt, 6'2", and Gene White, 5'11".

The 26-year-old Wood went to his "cat-and-mouse" game, spreading the floor in an attempt to create enough space for Plump or Ray Craft to drive to the basket and either shoot or pass to an open teammate. Milan jumped to a 25–17 lead at the half, but Muncie Central wore down its smaller opponent and moved in front,

28–26, by holding Milan without a basket in the third quarter. Seeing that momentum clearly had swung in favor of the bigger Muncie Central team, Wood decided to freeze the ball for most of the fourth quarter, even though his team trailed by two points.

"Everybody was going crazy wondering what was going on out there," said Plump, who stood and held the ball for four minutes, 14 seconds, to the amazement of the crowd at the Butler Fieldhouse. "We're behind in the tournament and yet we're holding the ball. I looked over at Coach Wood, and he's just sitting there nonchalantly."

"We felt if we could hang in there toward the end of the game, our experience would finally pay off," said Wood, who conceded that while Plump was holding the ball, he was trying to dream up some way for Milan to get back in front. "We had to do everything we could to conserve what energy we had to give us a chance at the end of the game, so we slowed it down earlier than we ever had."

When Milan finally came out of its stall, Plump missed a jump shot, but Muncie turned the ball over against the press, and Craft tied the score with a jumper. Milan went ahead, 30–28, on two free throws by Plump with 1:42 left, but Muncie's Gene Flowers responded with a basket to tie the score. Plump then held the ball until there were 18 seconds left, when he signaled for another timeout.

Wood set up the play: "Pass the ball to Plump," he said. "When Bobby crosses the line, everybody else clear to one side, away from him. Bobby, with about eight seconds to go, you start for the basket. Drive or shoot a jump shot, but don't shoot too early or they will have time to get another shot."

Plump crossed midcourt and with five seconds left started his move against Jimmy Barnes, who at 5'10" was about the same size as Plump. He faked left and drove right, creating enough daylight so he could pull up for a jumper from about 15 feet. It sailed through at the buzzer, giving Milan a 32–30 victory and the state championship.

"Now that I look back on it, I'm not so sure it wasn't destiny," said Wood.

The 1954 Milan High School basketball team is all smiles after what many regard as the greatest high school upset victory of all time. Coach Marvin Wood is at right.

Hollywood, a place that trades on dreams and miracles, eventually made a movie based on the Milan Miracle. Titled *Hoosiers* (MGM, 1986), it starred Gene Hackman as coach Norman Dale.

42

The Deflection

April 16, 1954, the Olympia, Detroit

After one period in the grand finale of their back-and-forth seven-game Stanley Cup Finals series against the Detroit Red Wings, the Montreal Canadiens must have been thinking sweet thoughts of bringing the Stanley Cup back to their hockey-crazy city. Ahead by a score of 1–0, the team from Montreal seemed to have momentum firmly entrenched on their side of the ice.

The Red Wings had finished the regular season seven points ahead of the defending champs, but Montreal had swept past the Boston Bruins in the semifinal round while the Red Wings had dropped only one game to the Toronto Maple Leafs. In addition, the Canadiens had proven in the regular season to be the more dangerous offensive unit, led as always by their skilled yet volatile superstar, Maurice "the Rocket" Richard.

And now all Montreal goalie Gerry McNeil, who had started Games 5 and 6 in place of rookie Jacques Plante, needed to do to become Montreal's hero was hold his team's lead for two periods. This was due to the scoring prowess of Floyd Curry, who put a 50-foot shot on Detroit's sensational goalie, Terry Sawchuk, at 9:17 of the first stanza. The puck made it through traffic in front of the Red Wings goal to bounce over the stick of Detroit's nearly impenetrable netminder, giving the

> ## "You've just seen the sweetest balanced team I've ever watched in my 35 years in hockey."
>
> —Red Wings coach Tommy Ivan

Canadiens a lead that they hoped to ride all the way to the Cup.

The Red Wings had other ideas, however, and came out firing in the second period. With Montreal's Paul Masnick serving time for a hooking penalty, Detroit took to the power play in hope of netting the tying goal. Using the precision attack for which they had become famous, Detroit's Ted Lindsay spotted Red Wings defenseman Red Kelly alone to the left of McNeil's crease. Lindsay whipped a sharp pass through the Montreal defense, which Kelly gathered in and converted at the 1:17 mark of the second period. The game stood tied at one apiece as the 15,792 Hockey Town fans let the foes from across the border know that they truly were in enemy territory.

Despite the support of the hometown faithful, the frantic pace that Detroit had maintained throughout the first two periods caught up with them at the beginning of the third. The Canadiens mounted a furious attack on the tiring Wings, and Detroit coach Tommy Ivan found he was unable to put together a line of rested players. As Montreal's potent offense unleashed its fury on Detroit's beleaguered corps, however, the Red Wings found that their last line of defense was in fact their best. Sawchuk was unbeatable, turning away each and every shot that the Canadiens sent in his direction. His most impressive play, and perhaps the defining play of the series, came early in that frantic third period when Montreal's Gaye Stewart found himself alone on a breakaway. Sawchuk, ever ready in goal, calmly turned aside the best scoring chance the Canadiens had seen all game and in doing so reinvigorated his fatigued teammates.

Another key moment came at the 16-minute mark of the final regulation period, as Richard ruined a likely scoring chance for the Canadiens. With the puck loose in front of the Detroit goal, Richard was unable to get his stick on it and instead picked the disk up and threw it past Sawchuk. Referee Bill Chadwick clearly saw the infraction and disallowed what would have been the go-ahead goal for Montreal. Making Richard's blunder even more costly was the fact that fellow Canadien Elmer Latch was in prime position to legally deposit the puck into the Detroit net.

Instead the two teams went into overtime play. At 4:29 of the sudden-death overtime period, the Red Wings took back the Cup in sudden and unlikely fashion. Tony Leswick, who generally held the job of chasing down the opposition's highest scorers, shot the puck from 40 feet away toward a crowd in front of the Montreal net. Unthinkably, the puck caromed off of Canadiens defenseman Doug Henry and over McNeil's shoulder.

The puck found the back of the net, and Detroit refound the title that it had held four of the previous five NHL seasons. The Red Wings, trailing 1–0 after a period of play, having blown a 3–1 series lead, had responded with a breathtaking and improbable victory in the deciding game of the series, once again proving themselves worthy of the title of Stanley Cup champions.

The Red Wings appeared sluggish during the extra frame, and the Cup appeared ripe for the Montreal taking. The Canadiens, however, deflated by the play of Terry Sawchuk (right) and the mental mistake of Maurice Richard (top), were unable to mount a threatening attack.

43

Fred Brown's Pass

March 29, 1982, Louisiana Superdome, New Orleans

Long before he became Air Jordan, when he was still a skinny freshman at the University of North Carolina, Michael Jordan wrote the first chapter in what would be a storybook career by hitting the game-winning shot against Georgetown in the 1982 NCAA championship game.

The game was a classic, close throughout. Georgetown's 7'0" freshman center, Patrick Ewing, started by swatting away just about anything that approached the basket, and North Carolina's first four baskets came on goaltending calls—it would be eight minutes before the Tar Heels would actually get the ball through the net.

Georgetown led 32–31 at halftime, and neither team led by more than four points in a tense, taut second half. A short jumper in the lane by Eric "Sleepy" Floyd gave Georgetown a 62–61 lead with 57 seconds left to play. North Carolina ran 25 seconds off the clock and then called a timeout to set up the play. All-American forward James Worthy, who

had scored 28 points and had made 13 of 17 field-goal attempts, seemed the most likely candidate to get the ball, because if he didn't hit his shot, he might well draw a foul. Instead, North Carolina coach Dean Smith opted to use Worthy as a decoy and have Jordan take the shot.

"They were all covered so I tried to pass it to Eric Smith, but it wasn't him."

—Georgetown guard Fred Brown

"I expected Georgetown to come back to the zone and jam it in," said Smith. "As it turned out, Michael's whole side of the court was wide open because they were chasing James."

James Black, North Carolina's point guard, faked a pass into the pivot and then found Jordan to the left of the basket, not far from the baseline. "I was all kinds of nervous," admitted Jordan, "but I didn't have time to think about doubts."

Jordan just did what he would do so many times over the next two decades:

he hit the big shot, sinking a 16-foot jumper with 15 seconds remaining to give North Carolina a 63–62 lead. "I didn't look at the ball at all," said Jordan. "I just prayed. I had a feeling it was going in, but I didn't see it go in. That shot put me on the basketball map."

But there were still 15 seconds left, and now it was Georgetown's turn. Sophomore point guard Fred Brown brought the ball upcourt and sought to set up a shooter. He first looked to the left baseline for Floyd, but the North Carolina defense was overplaying him. Brown next turned to the middle of the floor, hoping to feed Ewing or Ed Spriggs in the pivot. But there was a cluster of bodies in the lane and Brown didn't want to risk an entry pass.

With everyone else covered, Brown figured senior Eric Smith would be open on the right wing. "I thought I saw Smitty out of the right corner of my eye," Brown said. "My peripheral vision is pretty good, but this time it failed me. It was only a split second, but that's all it takes to lose a game."

The player Brown thought was Smith turned out to be Worthy, and Brown's pass went straight to the North Carolina forward. No one in the crowd of 61,612 at the Louisiana Superdome, nor among the millions watching on television, was more shocked than Worthy himself.

"I thought he'd try to lob it over me or throw it away from me," Worthy said. "I was surprised that it was right in my chest."

Worthy caught the pass with five seconds left and dribbled three seconds off the clock before Smith could catch him and foul him. Worthy missed both free throws, but it didn't matter because Georgetown only had time for a desperation heave by Floyd that was off target.

As the North Carolina players celebrated their victory, the 6'10" Georgetown coach, John Thompson, wrapped a protective arm around Brown and tried to console the player whose turnover had ended the team's chances. Asked what his coach said to him, Brown replied, "He told me that I had won more games for him than I had lost. He said not to worry."

Afterward, during the postgame interviews, Brown put the play in its proper perspective. "This is part of growing up," he said. "It was a great game. I loved playing it. I just wish the score was reversed at the end."

DEAN SMITH WINS FIRST TITLE

Six times in his illustrious career North Carolina coach Dean Smith had taken the Tar Heels to the Final Four, and six times he had come up empty. But for Smith, seven would be his lucky number.

Smith's first trip to the Final Four was in 1967, when North Carolina dropped an overtime decision to Dayton in the semifinals. His Tar Heels reached the Finals in 1968, losing to UCLA; the semifinals in 1969, losing to Purdue; the semifinals in 1972, losing to Florida State; the Finals in 1977, losing to Marquette; and the Finals in 1981, losing to Indiana.

But 1982 would be different. North Carolina entered the Final Four ranked number one in the nation with a 30–2 record, a talented team that featured All-American forward James Worthy, sophomore center Sam Perkins, and a flashy freshman by the name of Michael Jordan. For Smith, who would coach North Carolina to an NCAA Division I–record 879 victories in 36 seasons before retiring in 1997, this would be the team to get him to the top.

It did not come easily. In the semifinals, North Carolina posted a 68–63 victory over a Houston team on the rise that featured Clyde Drexler and a young Hakeem Olajuwon. And in the Finals, it went down to the last 15 seconds before Jordan's jumper and Worthy's steal gave North Carolina a 63–62 win over Georgetown and the title.

"This is one we'll always remember," said Worthy, who was chosen Most Outstanding Player of the Final Four. "It was the one that made us and Dean Smith champions."

After the game, Smith savored his first NCAA championship—he would win a second one 11 years later, in 1992–93—and held up a string from one of the nets that had been cut down in the celebration. "I got my net," he declared, beaming. "Sitting on the bench it really was just another game, but now it's not."

John Thompson, Georgetown University's basketball coach, talks with player Fred Brown.

From left to right: the Tar Heels' Michael Jordan, Matt Doherty, Sam Perkins, and their coach, Dean Smith.

44

Runaway Rose

July 14, 1970, Riverfront Stadium, Cincinnati

Like good manners and fins on cars, the All-Star Game used to matter. The game meant more to ballplayers than just the chance to earn an incentive clause in their contract. The game pitted the best players of one league against the best of the other, and players took pride in their leagues. They battled. For many, it was the biggest game of the year, and the competitive juices flowed. The selections were made by their fellow players, and it was not purely a popularity contest. The respect of their peers was a big deal indeed. Despite his countless heroic deeds, Ted Williams always claimed that his 1941 All-Star Game homer was his proudest moment, and the photo of pin-striped Joe DiMaggio greeting him at home plate says it all.

Back when it mattered there were some wonderful midsummer classics, perhaps none with a more dramatic finish than the 1970 game at Riverfront Stadium, where local Cincinnati Red Pete Rose slammed full force into Cleveland Indians catcher Ray Fosse in the bottom of the twelfth inning to win the game for the Nationals, breaking a 4–4 tie as he prevented Fosse from taking the throw from center that would have put Rose out at the plate.

The American Leaguers really wanted to win this one. They'd lost seven All-Star Games in a row. It was a humbling streak

> ## "Nobody told me they changed it to girls softball between third and home."
>
> —Pete Rose

dating back to 1963 (although not as humiliating as the 11-game losing streak they suffered from 1972 through 1982).

Neither team managed a run until the AL put one across in the sixth, and they added another in the seventh. It was Fosse who scored on Carl Yastrzemski's single in the sixth, and it was Fosse who drove in the run in the seventh with a sacrifice fly. Although the NL scored once in the bottom of the seventh, the Americans added two more in the eighth, courtesy of a Brooks Robinson triple. With the score at 4–1, it was looking good for the AL going into the bottom of the ninth.

No curtain call yet, however, as the National Leaguers scored three times in the bottom of the ninth to send the game into extra innings. Neither team scored in the tenth, nor did they in the eleventh, nor did Commissioner Bowie Kuhn declare the game a tie and send everyone packing.

In the twelfth, Claude Osteen pitched his third inning of scoreless ball for the NL, and Clyde Wright of the Angels (seventh pitcher of the night for the AL) got the first two batters out in the bottom of the inning. Then Pete Rose singled.

The Dodgers' Billy Grabarkewitz singled, too. First and second, two outs, and Jim Hickman of the Cubs, already 0-for-3 on the night, drove a single to center on a 1–0 pitch. As Amos Otis' throw sailed in from center, Rose motored full steam around third, bowling over Fosse, who stood between him and the plate.

The moving object—Rose—lowered his shoulder and struck the stationary object—Fosse—with enough power to knock the stocky catcher off his feet and knock the catcher's mitt off his hand. Fosse never had the ball. It hit him, and as it rolled all the way to the backstop, Rose flipped over, slapping his hand on home plate to win the game. "I thought I hit a mountain," Rose said of Fosse after the game.

Rose was hurt on the play and had to sit out the next three games, but Fosse was back in the Indians' lineup without missing a game. He played until he broke his finger a couple of months later in the season. He played through pain, though: the following spring an x-ray determined that his shoulder had been fractured in the collision with Rose.

"Don't tell me it's an exhibition," Rose said. "If I play a charity softball game for nothing—not a dime—I go all out. That's the only way I know how to play."

Was it an unfair hit? That's been debated for decades. Some think it was unnecessary, an excess by Charlie Hustle. Frank Robinson, Rose's former teammate, reportedly told his AL colleague Frank Howard, "He didn't have to do that to Fosse." But the manager of the American League team, Earl Weaver, defended Rose: "That's definitely the only way to play. You play to win. You don't compromise." That's why they call them All-Stars.

COLLISION COURSE

Ray Fosse was never the same after the collision at the plate. Even today his shoulder hurts him, so badly at times that the A's broadcaster sometimes declines to play golf for fear he'd not be able to finish the full 18 holes.

Fosse was hitting .313 and had 16 homers at the All-Star break in 1970. After the break (his shoulder was fractured, though he didn't know it at the time), he finished the season hitting .307, but with only two more home runs. He was never the same player again, although he stuck in the majors for eight more years. "I had the swing in the first half of that year you dream about having the rest of your career. I never got it back. I was never the offensive player from that point," Fosse lamented. He did taste glory; he played in three postseasons for the Oakland A's from 1973 to 1975, winning World Series rings in 1973 and 1974.

Pete Rose, of course, is baseball's all-time leader in base hits, with 4,256. But the hero of the night wound up doing time for income tax evasion in 1990 at the United States penitentiary situated in Ray Fosse's hometown of Marion, Illinois. Whatever he did off the field, however, Rose played hardball between the lines.

The National League's Pete Rose (No. 14, above) is hugged by teammate Dick Dietz after scoring the winning run.

Rose slams into catcher Ray Fosse, scoring the winning run to break a 4–4 tie in the bottom of the twelfth inning during the 1970 All-Star Game in Cincinnati.

45

Webber's Timeout

April 5, 1993, Louisiana Superdome, New Orleans

It was an illustrious year for the Final Four. Three out of the four teams were number one seeds in 1993; the other was a number two. North Carolina knocked off second-seeded Kansas, while Michigan beat Kentucky in overtime to create a matchup of two of the country's top-ranked teams for the championship.

Both teams felt confident that they could win. In fact, both felt the championship *belonged* to them. No question about it. There were good arguments in favor of each.

Michigan played in the final game in 1992, losing to Duke. Throughout the 1993 season, the Wolverines remembered that game and what it felt like to be one of the last two teams playing. It was great to be back, and they wanted to make this one count.

North Carolina wanted the win for an entirely different reason. They were coming off a particularly poor 1992 season in which they lost nine games and were eliminated from the NCAA Tournament in the regional semifinals. This was their opportunity to redeem

themselves and prove they were indeed champions.

Tar Heels coach Dean Smith would deny it, but he may have felt the pressure more than anyone. He had the most coaching victories in NCAA Tournaments (55) and had taken more teams to the tournament than any other college coach,

> ## "It made me grow up a lot faster than if it hadn't happened."
>
> —Michigan forward Chris Webber

with 23. He guided eight teams all the way to the Final Four, but in all those years only one North Carolina team won the championship.

The teams were fairly evenly matched in 1993, with a wealth of quality players. Amidst some recruiting criticism, Smith came through with a stellar class in 1990. Sports analysts touted the group as one of the finest freshman classes in recruiting history. Unfortunately, Clifford Rozier transferred to Louisville after his

freshman season, and the nation turned its attention to Michigan's 1991 Fab Five freshman class, now sophomores.

This wasn't the first time that these two teams met this season. In December's Rainbow Classic tournament in Hawaii, Michigan beat North Carolina, 79–78, on a Jalen Rose shot at the buzzer. Far from being disheartened, the Tar Heels had a newfound confidence after the game. Coming off a disappointing season, they were able to hold their own against a team that had played in the 1992 championship game.

Michigan may have had the upper hand in raw talent. They were agile and physically gifted, but the Tar Heels countered with an offensive ball movement made up of intricate patterns. The momentum went back and forth. Michigan leaped to a 23–11 first-quarter lead, but North Carolina came back with a 42–36 lead at the half.

A crowd of 64,151 watched as each team took control only to lose it again. With 15 minutes left to play, North Carolina was up, 53–46, but with 4:31 left on the clock, it was Michigan on top,

67–63. Three minutes ticked by while the Tar Heels racked up nine points and Michigan missed three shots and gave up a turnover.

In fact, Michigan's Jalen Rose had six turnovers for the game, but it was this last that proved the most disastrous. George Lynch took control of the ball for the Tar Heels and passed off to an open Eric Montross, who got the dunk to give North Carolina a 72–67 lead with just 1:03 to go.

But it wasn't over. Ray Jackson hit a corner jumper, bringing the Wolverines to within three. Then Brian Reese of North Carolina stepped on the sideline while fielding an inbounds pass, and the ball belonged to Michigan. Rose's shot missed, but Chris Webber got the offensive rebound and the basket, closing the gap to 72–71.

Junior Pat Sullivan, a North Carolina reserve forward, was fouled on the next play, and he went to the line, shooting two. Above the taunts of Wolverines players lined up along the paint, Sullivan sunk the first shot but missed the second.

Webber grabbed the rebound and dribbled toward the Wolverines bench where he called a timeout with 11 seconds left on the clock. The only problem was that Michigan had no timeouts left. A technical foul was called on the Wolverines, and Donald Williams was sent to the line for North Carolina. He made all four shots, sealing the 77–71 win and the championship for the Tar Heels.

THE CONTROVERSIAL TIMEOUT CALL

Years after the 1993 NCAA basketball championship, memories blurred concerning the specifics of that game. No one would be surprised that North Carolina won, since they are renowned as a basketball powerhouse. In fact, North Carolina went to the Final Four three times from 1991 to 1994.

Many basketball fans would remember 1993 as the year that Michigan's Fab Five were sophomores with enough talent to go all the way to the title match. This was the last year the five would all play on the same court.

But what most people still remember about that 1993 championship is Michigan Wolverine Chris Webber's controversial—and illegal—timeout call with no timeouts left.

There has been a lot of speculation about the play. For their part, the North Carolina players were stunned. "It is something I don't think would happen to us," said George Lynch. "Coach Smith had us better prepared."

Pat Sullivan, who sunk one of two Tar Heels free throws just before the call, agreed. "We were not allowed to call for timeouts unless Coach Smith was calling for one. At Carolina, timeouts are like gold."

And Eric Montross added, "Don't blame Chris Webber. Blame the coaches. They all should have known better."

But Michigan coach Steve Fisher said he actually mentioned the timeout situation at the last break. "I guess we didn't get the situation explained clearly enough."

After it was all over, Webber himself wasn't clear on what happened. "I don't remember," he said. "Just called a timeout and we didn't have a timeout. And I cost our team the game."

But Pat Sullivan takes exception to that, stressing that North Carolina's win shouldn't be tarnished by Webber's mistake. "Michigan would still have had to come down the court and make a shot," he said. "Hopefully the timeout is not what people think cost Michigan the game. It obviously helped us, but it didn't determine the outcome of the game."

And if you don't already know, the mishap didn't hurt Webber's future in basketball. He left college after his sophomore year and was a first-round draft pick.

Chris Webber (No. 4, above left) stands by as Eric Montross celebrates during North Carolina's technical foul shots in the final seconds. Michigan was assessed a technical foul after Webber erroneously called a timeout. Webber (left) blocks a shot by North Carolina's Eric Montross (No. 00). Michigan's Jalen Rose is in the background.

46

The Fight

February 18, 1979, Daytona International Speedway, Daytona Beach, Florida

On an ominously dark and rainy day, the 1979 Daytona 500 began under the yellow caution flag and remained that way for a full 16 laps. Then, with patches of the track still damp from the rain that had for the moment abated, the green flag flew, and the race that CBS had chosen as the first Daytona ever to be televised from start to finish was under way.

Immediately, it was clear that there was something wrong with race-favorite Buddy Baker's car. Unable to make use of the power that his Oldsmobile had displayed in the 125-mile qualifying race, he quickly lost ground. By the 38th lap of the race, Baker was finished, done in by a loose wire in his engine, which ended up blowing a cylinder on the very first lap.

But the drama on the track was just beginning. Cale Yarborough, Bobby Allison, and Donnie Allison were jostling for position at the front of the pack. Going into the first turn on the 32nd lap of the race, the Allison boys were out in front, and Yarborough was right behind them, desperately looking for an opening.

However, during the turn, Bobby brushed up against his younger brother, sending both cars, along with Yarborough's, off the track and onto the sodden infield grass. No major damage

> ## "Cale had made up his mind he would pass me low, and I had my mind made up he was going to have to pass me high."
> ### —driver Donnie Allison

was done to the three cars, but they all lost significant time. Donnie Allison lost one lap, while Bobby Allison lost two and Yarborough dropped three behind the leading group. This was not the last time these three would meet in this problem-marred race.

Over the next 50 laps the lead changed hands 14 times, with Dale Earnhardt, Benny Parsons, and Richard Petty all temporarily holding the lead.

Meanwhile, Donnie Allison and Yarborough were creeping back into the race. One by one, the two determined drivers took advantage of crashes and engine failures to make up the laps they had lost.

With just 10 laps to go, not only had Donnie Allison and Yarborough made up their laps, but they now held the lead. Allison was out in front, but the wily Yarborough was waiting for the opportunity to make a move for the lead. The two had a 20-second lead on the trio of A. J. Foyt, Richard Petty, and Darrell Waltrip, who were engaged in a furious struggle for third place.

Just four laps from the finish line, Petty and Waltrip passed Foyt for third. They also closed the substantial distance between themselves and the two Oldsmobiles struggling for the lead. The final lap saw Yarborough close the small gap between himself and Allison. Going into the backstretch, Yarborough mistook Ralph Jones, who had been lapped and was slowing down and running low on the track to get out of the leaders' way, for

Bobby Allison. Yarborough immediately assumed the elder Allison was setting up to help Donnie.

Coming out of Turn 2, Yarborough made a decisive move to get past Donnie Allison by going low on the track. Allison, however, had the same idea. Both drivers stuck to their plans, and just before Turn 3 the two cars came together. Yarborough found himself on the grass and promptly lost control. Allison, who was also trying to run low, couldn't escape Yarborough's careering car, and he too was swept up the track.

In one stunning moment, the leaders had wrecked and were now skidding along the wall high on Turn 3. Petty couldn't believe his eyes as he came around the turn. He had pulled out in front of Waltrip and now found himself very suddenly in the lead. The crowd favorite turned his attention to holding off the determined young driver behind him, which he did, beating Waltrip by one car length. The 120,000 in attendance that day were on their feet, roaring as Petty crossed the finish line and the checkered flag waved.

Meanwhile, a fight ensued on Turn 3 as Yarborough and Bobby Allison, who had stopped to check on his brother, exchanged blows. To all this, however, Petty was oblivious. He took his crew and went in joyous fashion to Daytona's victory lane for the sixth time in his career. Only 18 cars had emerged from a race that started with 41, and Petty had finished first among them. The first Daytona 500 ever to be broadcast live had certainly given every viewer, at the track and at home, a spellbinding example of auto racing at its most exciting.

THE 1979 DAYTONA 500—WHAT A MESS!

- Buddy Baker was forced out with a blown cylinder.
- David Pearson, Joe Millikan, and others were involved in a six-car crash and were finished for the day. Soon after, Darrell Waltrip lost a cylinder, but managed to stay with Richard Petty, who had earlier lost a cylinder of his own.
- Neil Bonnett blew a tire and spun off Turn 4.
- Rookie Harry Gant was hit by Ricky Rudd and sent hard into the infield guardrail, ending his day.
- John Utsman's engine blew in the Trioval.
- Benny Parsons lost his lead to Donnie Allison as one of his cylinder heads cracked.
- Blackie Wangerin blew his engine, and Dave Marcis crashed in the resulting oil spill.
- Paul Fess blew his engine.
- Tighe Scott blew his chance at the lead by sliding three stalls too far while attempting to pit.
- Dale Earnhardt similarly lost his chance at victory when he overrevved his engine, thus breaking a cylinder and dislodging his hood.
- Donnie Allison and Cale Yarborough crashed on the backstretch of the final lap, setting up a win by Richard Petty and a fistfight between Yarborough and Donnie's older brother, Bobby Allison.

Bobby Allison (left) stands over Cale Yarborough after the collision. Allison was leading the race before the mishap.

Van de Velde's Collapse

July 15-18, 1999, Carnoustie Golf Links, Scotland

Paul *who*? At the 1999 British Open, a little-known Scotsman came out of nowhere—10 strokes out of the lead in the final round—to hoist the claret jug at Carnoustie Golf Links. Then ranked 159th in the world, Paul Lawrie became the first Scotsman to win the coveted British Open on Scottish soil since Tommy Armour at Carnoustie in 1931. His remarkable come-from-behind victory was ultimately overshadowed, however, by Jean Van de Velde's spectacular collapse on the eighteenth hole.

Carnoustie Golf Links has long been regarded as one of the most challenging golf courses in the world. Walter Hagen reportedly considered it the greatest golf course in the British Isles. Others have been more critical in their assessment of the wind-swept course, which has been dubbed the "killer links" and "Car-nasty." Phil Mickelson, along with Sergio Garcia, Vijay Singh, and defending champion Mark O'Meara, had failed to make the cut. In fact, nearly 30 percent of the field had been unable to break 80 in the first two rounds. Even Tiger Woods, who had placed third in the 1998 tournament, was off his game. As more and more players fell prey to the course's treacherous mix of high winds and heavy rough, the Open began to resemble a game of dominoes.

In the final round, an unlikely leader emerged from the field: French-born Jean

> ## "All it proves is that I was capable of being 3 ahead of the best players in the world on eighteen."
> ## —Jean Van de Velde

Van de Velde, who had not won a tournament since 1993's Roma Masters, held a 10-stroke lead over Lawrie. American Justin Leonard, the 1997 British Open champion, also remained a contender for his second British Open title. Meanwhile, Lawrie surprised everyone by ending the day with a final-round score of 67 and 4 under par. With an overall score of 290—the same as Leonard, who shot 72 for his final round—

Lawrie retired to the clubhouse to watch Van de Velde tee off at the eighteenth hole. Even if Van de Velde made a colossal blunder and double-bogeyed the hole, his victory was assured.

With a 3-stroke lead over Lawrie and Leonard, Van de Velde teed off at the par-4, 487-yard-long eighteenth hole. The ball swerved more than 20 yards to the right of the fairway, cleared the water, and landed in the low rough. So far, so good. But before you could say "Vive la France," Van de Velde made the fateful decision to use a 2-iron rather than a sand wedge. With the wedge, he could have chipped the ball back onto the fairway, hit an approach shot to the green, and then 2-putted for the championship. Instead, disaster struck.

Going for the green, Van de Velde sent the ball right into the grandstand in front of the creek. The ball bounced back across the water into knee-high rough. Van de Velde's chances for an easy victory suddenly began to dim.

His third shot drew stunned gasps from the crowd. The ball flew out of the rough and into the water. Van de Velde now had to make a choice: either take a penalty stroke or play the ball from the water. After removing his shoes and rolling up his pants, Van de Velde waded into the water to take a shot. But as the ball sank deeper into the sand, he reconsidered and took the 1-stroke-penalty drop instead. The ball cleared the water, only to land in the front green–side bunker; Van de Velde's nightmare wasn't over yet. Fortunately, his bunker shot landed 10 feet to the left of the eighteenth hole. He then sank the putt for a triple bogey 7—good enough for a spot in the playoff against Lawrie and Leonard. Van de Velde's humiliation was now complete. In approximately 15 minutes, he had blown his 3-stroke lead with his triple bogey 7 on the eighteenth hole. As the skies opened up over Carnoustie, he joined Lawrie and Leonard at the fifteenth hole to begin the aggregate-stroke playoff for the title.

The playoff got off to a rocky start, as all three bogeyed the fifteenth and sixteenth holes (Van de Velde actually *double-bogeyed* the fifteenth). On the 459-yard-long seventeenth hole, however, Lawrie took a 1-shot lead. The Aberdeen native then pulled off a miracle at the eighteenth hole. With Van de Velde out of the running and Leonard's second shot floating in the creek, Lawrie took his second shot. The ball soared through the air and landed four feet from the hole.

The rain-drenched crowd exploded into cheers and applause as Lawrie sank the putt to win the British Open. Not since the 1956 Masters, when Jackie Burke Jr. came from 8 strokes behind to defeat Ken Venturi, had a golfer made such an astonishing comeback in a major tournament. Yet, for all the hoopla surrounding Lawrie's surprise victory, Van de Velde's epic fall was the talk of the golf world. Few golfers had ever self-destructed to such an embarrassing degree in a major tournament. Even as Lawrie savored his victory, his heart went out to Van de Velde: "I feel sorry for Jean. He really should have won. Thankfully for me, he didn't."

As for Van de Velde, he took his loss with admirable sangfroid: "Maybe next time I'll be better able to handle the pressure. It's difficult, but there are worse things in life."

THE 1999 BRITISH OPEN TOURNAMENT

Playoff Scores

Player	15th Hole	16th Hole	17th Hole	18th Hole	Total
Paul Lawrie	5	4	3	3	15
Justin Leonard	5	4	4	5	18
Jean Van de Velde	6	4	3	5	18

Final Standings—Top Players

Rank	Player	R1	R2	R3	R4	Total	Par	Money
1	Paul Lawrie	73	74	76	67	290	6	$577,500
2T	Justin Leonard	73	74	71	72	290	6	$305,250
2T	Jean Van de Velde	75	68	70	77	290	6	$305,250
4T	Angel Cabrera	75	69	77	70	291	7	$165,000
4T	Craig Parry	76	75	67	73	291	7	$165,000
6	Greg Norman	76	70	75	72	293	9	$115,500
7T	David Frost	80	69	71	74	294	10	$82,500
7T	Davis Love III	74	74	77	69	294	10	$82,500
7T	Tiger Woods	74	72	74	74	294	10	$82,500
10T	Scott Dunlap	72	77	76	70	295	11	$57,420
10T	Jim Furyk	78	71	76	70	295	11	$57,420
10T	Retief Goosen	76	75	73	71	295	11	$57,420
10T	Jesper Parnevik	74	71	78	72	295	11	$57,420
10T	Hal Sutton	73	78	72	72	295	11	$57,420

Jean Van de Velde smiles during the final round as he stands in the water of the Barry Burn that crosses the 18th fairway to see if his ball was playable. Van de Velde went on to make triple-bogey and lose the Open in a playoff. But he hasn't stopped smiling since, a trait that has endeared him to fans and given his golfing career a major boost.

48

Wimbledon Marathon

July 3, 1970, All-England Club, Wimbledon, England

The long-simmering rivalry between Margaret Smith Court and Billie Jean King came to a thrilling head at the 1970 Wimbledon women's final. Over the course of two hours and 28 minutes—the longest women's final in the tournament's history—the two players waged a dramatic battle for the title.

When it was over, Court held the Wimbledon trophy up before the cheering spectators, but only after defeating King in a match that prompted normally staid sportswriters to wax poetic. As one writer described it in The Times, "The match had a thrilling beauty that chilled the blood."

Hyperbole aside, the 1970 Wimbledon women's final featured two of the era's finest players competing at the peak of their game. Known as the Arm for her extraordinary reach, Margaret Smith Court dominated women's tennis during the sixties. Nearly 6'0" tall, the Australian-born Court lifted weights daily to build strength and endurance. At 18, she won the first of her 11 Australian Open titles in 1960. Although shy and devoutly

religious, Court was ultracompetitive and driven on the court, to the point that she often played when ill—and won. In 1961, she made her Wimbledon debut in the doubles final, where she and partner Jan Lehane lost to Karen Hentze and newcomer Billie Jean King, née Moffitt. Bouncing back from that defeat, Court

"Champions keep playing until they get it right."
—Billie Jean King

took her first Wimbledon singles title in 1963 against King in a match lasting all of 51 minutes. Then, in rapid-fire succession, she began accumulating Grand Slam titles, including seven consecutive Australian Opens, from 1960 to 1967.

By all standards, Margaret Smith Court was the world's number one woman player in the sixties, but one goal still eluded her: winning all four majors in the calendar year. As of 1970, the only female player to have accomplished this Grand Slam was Maureen "Little Mo" Connolly, back in 1953. Court had nearly pulled it off in 1962, 1965, and 1969. Now, with

victories in the 1970 Australian and French Opens behind her, Court planned to make it three-for-three at Wimbledon, as long as her nerves didn't sabotage her game.

Unlike Court, Billie Jean King seemed to relish the spotlight. Born and raised in Long Beach, California, King was an all-around athlete who found an early mentor in tennis great Alice Marble. Under Marble's guidance, King quickly rose through the ranks to win the 1961 Wimbledon doubles final with Karen Hantze. An extroverted player who frequently shouted or punched the air during tournaments, King soon emerged as the only real threat to Court's dominance of sixties-era women's tennis. After her humiliating loss to Court in the 1963 Wimbledon singles final, King won the title three years in a row, from 1966 to 1968. No longer the unseeded 20-year-old who faced Court in 1963, King was ready to square off against her longtime rival in the 1970 Wimbledon final.

Prior to the final, Court sprained her left ankle so severely that she defaulted in the two doubles events. Shot full of pain-killers, she nonetheless took to the court for the showdown with King, who decided to exploit Court's injury to her advantage. In the early games of the first set, King used a combination of drop shots and lobs to keep Court running between the net and baseline. This strategy initially appeared to work, and King broke Court's service to take the lead at 5–4. Just as King served for the set, however, Court rallied to make it 5 all. Whatever hopes King had for an easy victory dissipated, as Court repeatedly broke King's serve for the first set. When Court broke King's serve to make it 8 all, King slammed her racket on the ground in frustration. The first set dragged on, with no immediate end in sight. Finally, after nine more games, Court took the first set at 14–12. It had taken her only 26 games and 88 minutes!

Her left ankle taped for support, Court did not appear impeded by her injury. Nor had the marathon first set sapped her energy. Although King took the first game of the second set, Court again rallied to meet her opponent head-on. As the second set stretched to 20 games, an old knee injury began to trouble King. Suffering from muscle cramps, she fought off five match points, but despite King's superhuman efforts, the set ultimately went to Court, 11–9. In one of the most dramatic and hotly contested finals in the tournament's history, Aussie Margaret Smith Court won her third Wimbledon title. A few months later, she defeated Rosie Casals at the U.S. Open to realize her dream of completing the Grand Slam.

Margaret Smith Court (right, top and bottom) was the victor in the longest and most grueling women's final ever played at Wimbledon. The scores were 14–12, 11–9.

Billie Jean King (left) waves as she poses with her husband, Larry. King was a triple winner in the Wimbledon tennis championships.

49

Messier Guarantees Victory

May 25, 1994, Meadowlands Arena, East Rutherford, New Jersey

New York Rangers coach Mike Keenan had spent days letting Rangers fans know how banged up their heroes were and what exceptional hockey their foes from New Jersey had played to gain a 3–2 lead in the NHL Eastern Conference Finals. It was as if even Keenan knew how the show, which had been running for 53 consecutive Stanley Cup–less years, had to go and was already making excuses for the unavoidable ending. This was not what the long-suffering fans of New York needed. What they needed was a larger-than-life player who could rewrite the tired Rangers' script and deliver something magical. Enter Mark Messier and his now legendary guarantee.

"We know we have to win it," the Rangers captain said before Game 6. "We can win it. And we are going to win it."

Game 6 started in ominous fashion for the visiting Rangers, despite Messier's prediction, as the Devils jumped out to a 2–0 lead in the first period. New Jersey captain Scott Stevens had started the scoring on a fluke goal that ricocheted past Rangers goalie Mike Richter after bouncing off the stick of defenseman Sergei Nemchinov. Going into the second period, the Rangers looked like they'd already been beat.

> ## "We know we have to win it. We can win it. And we are going to win it."
> —Rangers captain Mark Messier

But Keenan, despite the excuses, wasn't going to go down without a fight. He moved promising second-year center Alexi Kovalev from his regular second-line center position onto the first line to play right wing next to Messier. Kovalev had thus far been held pointless in the series and had been lambasted in the New York media for being intimidated by the physical play of the Devils.

At 18:19 of the second period, however, Kovalev found himself in the clear for a slap shot, and whatever fear he felt of the rough New Jersey defense melted away as the puck found the back of the net behind the Devils' rookie goalie Martin Brodeur. From that instant on, Kovalev, having defeated his own demons, went to work on the ones in red and black who were attempting to hand the Rangers their 54th straight season sans the Cup.

At 2:48 of the third period, Kovalev rushed into the Devils zone and set up Messier on a nifty pass for the back-handed goal that tied up the game and proved to be the beginning of one of the greatest individual performances in the history of the NHL. Messier had made a bold promise before the game and, like Joe Namath and Muhammad Ali before him, now claimed the third period as his time to make good on it.

Ten minutes later, as the two teams were playing four men to a side, Kovalev once again unleashed his powerful slap shot on Brodeur, who managed this time to turn away the puck. However, Messier muscled himself into perfect position, and at 12:12 he struck the rebound past the helpless netminder and gave the Rangers an improbable 3–2 lead.

Finally, with Brodeur out for an extra attacker and less than two minutes remaining in the game, Messier helped himself to a natural hat trick by dumping the puck into the empty net to shut the door on the home team. The Rangers had survived a trip to hell by climbing on the shoulders of their commander in chief, and now the blue shirts could go back to Broadway for a deciding Game 7. The Devils, however, weren't turning tail just yet. Showing no signs of panic, they prepared to enter the lion's den that was Madison Square Garden and do battle one last time with the Rangers and their suddenly immortal leader.

The Rangers, who had won only one other Game 7 in their playoff history, had what seemed like all of New York City packed into the Garden to lend their raucous support. The roar of the crowd was deafening when Rangers defenseman Brian Leetch gave New York a 1–0 lead at 9:31 of the second period, and reached a crescendo when the Garden's PA system announced: "One minute to play in the game."

But with 7.7 seconds standing between the Rangers and a date with Vancouver, the Devils' Valery Zelepukin turned down the crowd's volume by beating Richter on a goal that left the Rangers keeper nearly speechless.

As stunning as Zelepukin's goal may have been, the grand finale of this legendary series was better. At 4:24 of the second overtime, the Rangers' Stephane Matteau beat Scott Niedermayer to a loose puck to Brodeur's right, skated behind the New Jersey net, and scored the game-winner on a flawless wrap-around goal.

The Garden reached unprecedented decibel levels as it voiced its approval. The Devils went home, and the Rangers went on to win the Stanley Cup for the first time since 1940. The guarantee was fulfilled, the script was rewritten, and a New York sports legend was born.

The New York Rangers' Adam Graves celebrates a goal by teammate and captain Mark Messier (right rear) against New Jersey Devils goaltender Martin Brodeur. Messier scored three third-period goals to lead the Rangers to a 4–2 win and to tie the finals at three games each.

TOO CLOSE FOR COMFORT: RANGERS-DEVILS 1994

Hockey is hardly the most relaxing game, but when the Rangers and the Devils faced off, there wasn't much time to relax and enjoy the game.

Game 1: Devils 4, Rangers 3
Claude Lemieux tied the game with 43 seconds remaining at Madison Square Garden. Stephane Richer beat the Rangers' Mike Richter to win the game in double overtime.

Game 2: Rangers 4, Devils 0
Mark Messier scored on the first shot of the game. The Rangers didn't look back and cruised to victory.

Game 3: Rangers 3, Devils 2
The Rangers sent 50 shots at Martin Brodeur, but it took a goal in double overtime by Stephane Matteau to win it for New York.

Game 4: Devils 3, Rangers 1
The Devils, without scorer Bernie Nicholls, triumphed over New York backup goalie Glenn Healy and the Rangers after Mike Keenan pulled Richter and benched several other Rangers regulars.

Game 5: Devils 4, Rangers 1
Nicholls' return doomed the Rangers as he netted two goals at Madison Square Garden. The Devils took a decisive 3–2 series advantage.

Game 6: Rangers 4, Devils 2
After guaranteeing the victory, Messier scored three goals in the third period to lift the Rangers to victory and stave off elimination.

Game 7: Rangers 2, Devils 1
At 4:24 of the second overtime, Matteau netted his second game-ender to send the Devils home and the Rangers into the finals against the Vancouver Canucks.

50

Kentucky Shootout

December 7, 2002, Fairgrounds Cardinal Stadium, Louisville, Kentucky

A crowd of 20,511 fans braved the bitter cold temperatures in Louisville, Kentucky, to attend the state's Class 4-A high school football championship.

The icy fans came to see the game between the two nationally ranked teams, but little did they know what sort of amazing event would unfold over the next three hours and 14 minutes on the frozen turf at Fairgrounds Cardinal Stadium. Instead of just seeing Trinity crowned state champion of Kentucky's largest classification for the 14th time in school history, the fans saw perhaps the best game ever played by two prep football teams.

The event that started as a football game turned into a video game–like offensive explosion that ended only when a little-known defensive player made a huge play to seal Louisville Trinity's 59–56 win over Louisville Male.

Trinity's Brian Brohm and Male's Michael Bush, two of the top prep quarterbacks in the country, shredded two defenses that had previously allowed only 278 points combined in their first 14 games for 1,337 yards of offense.

Receiver TaShawn McBroom had a state-final-best 300 yards receiving and three TDs on seven catches, and Daniel Mudd caught six passes for 201 yards and three TDs.

> ## "I thought it would be a mid-20 [point] game. But we had to come out and put it up. It was great."
>
> —Trinity quarterback Brian Brohm

Bush single-handedly brought Male back into the game after a 26–14 halftime deficit, and he played a huge part in the two teams combining for 40 third-quarter points. After his one-yard TD run early in the fourth quarter, Male recovered an onside kick. Four plays later, Bush hit Bryant Beck on a 14-yard touchdown pass to make it 52–49. Brohm and company then seemingly put the final dagger in Male's season with another touchdown. But the warrior named Bush—Kentucky's Mr. Football—wouldn't give up. He led his team on a seven-play, 80-yard drive and made it 59–56 on a 13-yard touchdown pass to Corey James with 1:24 left in the tilt.

And then the unthinkable happened. B. J. Adams came up with yet *another* onside kick, and Male had the ball with 1:21 left in the game, giving Bush one final shot. With the fans in a frenzy and Male just 45 yards away from the end zone and perhaps the wildest comeback in any prep event in Kentucky history, Bush took the ball and dropped back to the Male 46-yard line. He planted his left leg, cocked his left arm, and rifled a tight spiral to the right corner of the end zone.

There was a hush over the crowd as the ball traveled through the cold air. Running back Sergio Spencer broke free from a Trinity defender down the right sideline and for a split second Bush and his teammates could see themselves hoisting the trophy for their second title in three years. Brian Smith, who on Male's last possession had dropped an interception that could have virtually sealed the game, was the Trinity player Spencer had gotten two steps behind. "As the ball was in the air, everything was going through my mind," Smith said. "The whole season was riding on one play."

Bush's heave came up just short of Spencer and, after watching receivers from both teams run up and down the field untouched for most of the game, Smith fully extended his body toward the goal line. He reached up and plucked the ball out of the middle of the air and kept control of it as he pounded to the frozen ground on the 1-yard line with 1:11 left to play.

"I just happened to be in the right place at the right time," Smith said later. "I knew the ball was going in the air. Coach told us, 'Don't let anybody get behind you.' I just knew I had to make the play. I had to make it."

There were other stellar defensive plays that night, but, in a game totally overshadowed by the offenses, Smith made the only play that mattered.

In high school football, all standout players have one game they'll remember for a lifetime. But rarely do the two best players in one state—and two of the best the country has to offer—have their best effort in the same game.

But that's exactly what happened in the 2002 Kentucky High School Class 4-A state championship between Louisville Male and Louisville Trinity, two large schools that were both nationally ranked prior to the contest.

Trinity won, 59–56, but the story was the amazing play by the quarterbacks. Trinity junior Brian Brohm, a third-generation signal caller, was considered the best quarterback in the country for the class of 2004. Male senior Michael Bush was playing his first year at quarterback but was one of the top five recruits in America. He was named Kentucky's Mr. Football. The duo put on a show and put up some mind-boggling numbers.

The 6'4", 200-pound Brohm completed 19 of 25 passes for 552 yards—that's 29.1 yards a completion and 22.1 per attempt—and seven touchdowns. He also rushed nine times for 52 yards and a touchdown.

Brohm, whose father was quarterback at the University of Louisville and whose brother Jeff was a star at the University of Louisville before playing six years in the NFL, had an NFL rating of 157.08 for the game. The highest possible mark is 158.

"He's an NFL player," said Male coach Bob Redman, whose son Chris is a quarterback for the Baltimore Ravens. "He's a special, special young man."

But as good as Brohm was that night, Bush might have been better in defeat.

The 6'3", 225-pound Bush was named Student Sports National Player of the Week after amassing 608 yards of offense and staying on the field for 147 of 158 plays, as he also played defensive back.

Bush completed 33 of 47 passes for 468 yards and six touchdowns, while carrying the ball 24 times for 116 yards and a touchdown and recording seven tackles.

Trinity's quarterback, junior Brian Brohm, completed 19 of 25 passes for a career-high 552 yards and seven touchdowns.

Editorial Panel Responsible for Rankings

Tony Barnhart, author and journalist
Jack Clary, author
Frank Deford, author and commentator
Peter Golenbock, author
Bob Hammel, author and journalist
Jerome Holtzman, author and journalist
Fred Klein, author and journalist

Les Krantz, author
Jim McKay, commentator
Bill Nowlin, author
Phil Pepe, author
Rob Rains, author
Dale Ratermann, author and sports executive
Alex Sachare, author

Ken Samelson, editor
Sue Sveum, author
Dick Whittingham, author
Pat Williams, author and sports executive
Rick Wolff, author and editor

Contributing Authors

Jody Demling: "Kentucky High School Shootout" (page 146).

Andy Horner: "Miracle on Ice" (page 10); "The Fight of the Century" (page 64); "The Long Count" (page 80); "American Dream" (page 122); "Mr. Clutch Delivers" (page 126); "The Deflection" (page 130); "The Fight" (page 138); "Messier Guarantees Victory" (page 144).

Tim Knight: "Nicklaus' Sixth Green Jacket" (page 90); "Watson's Birdie Chip" (page 96); "Hogan's Triumphant Return" (page 102); "Borg's Fifth Straight Wimbledon Title" (page 120); "Van de Velde's Collapse" (page 140); "Wimbledon Marathon" (page 142).

Bill Nowlin: "The Shot Heard 'Round the World" (page 2); "Buckner's Boot" (page 48); "Slaughter's Mad Dash" (page 94); "The Rally Off Rivera" (page 98); "Henderson Stuns Halos" (page 108); "Runaway Rose" (page 134).

Jim Prime: "Maz Makes History" (page 26); "Fisk Waves It Fair" (page 34); "Gibson in a Pinch" (page 52); "Larsen's Perfect Game" (page 68); "Carter Crushes Philly" (page 116); "Merkle's Blunder" (page 124).

Rob Rains: "The Greatest Game Ever Played" (page 6); "The Immaculate Reception" (page 22); "Flutie's Hail Mary" (page 38); "The Comeback" (page 72); "A Game for the Ages" (page 76); "The Catch" (page 86); "The Drive" (page 88); "Lorenzo's Dunk" (page 92); "And the Band Played On" (page 100); "Montana's Super Drive" (page 104); "Notre Dame Stops the Streak" (page 110); "The Chicken Soup Game" (page 118).

Alex Sachare: "Havlicek's Steal" (page 44); "Laettner's Buzzer Beater" (page 56); "The Milan Miracle" (page 128); "Fred Brown's Pass" (page 132).

Sue Sveum: "Jordan's Parting Shot" (page 14); "The Ice Bowl" (page 18); "Munich Clock Controversy" (page 30); "Triple-Overtime Thriller" (page 60); "Smart's Swish" (page 112); "Affirmed's Triple Crown" (page 114); "Webber's Timeout" (page 136).

Photo Credits

All the photographs in this volume were provided by AP/Wide World Photos except the following:
Page 36: Bettman/Corbis
Page 46: Bettman/Corbis
Page 61: Bettman/Corbis
Page 64: Everett Collection
Page 111: Notre Dame
Page 129 (top): Indiana High School Athletic Association
Page 129 (bottom): Everett Collection
Page 147: the *Louisville Courier Journal*